CITIZEN SHEEP, GOVERNMENT SHEPHERDS

Mike Sodrel

Food For
Thought
PUBLISHING

www.mikesodrel.com

One Sodrel Drive
Jeffersonville, IN 47130

ISBN: 978-0-615-39029-1

Library of Congress Control Number: 2010904670

Printed in the United States of America

This book is printed on acid-free paper.

DEDICATION

I dedicate this book to Keta, my wife of 42 years, to our two children and their spouses, and to our seven grandchildren.

ACKNOWLEDGEMENTS

This book was written, edited, and designed in Southern Indiana. Thanks are extended to Allen Howie and the staff at Idealogy for the cover design, and to Tracy Powell for editing and designing the interior.

CONTENTS

FOREWORD

When I first decided to seek public office, a professional political consultant told me **campaigns are not about educating voters**. Campaigns, he said, are about winning elections. Frankly, I think they prefer it that way. **It is easier to manipulate people who do not understand government.**

This book is an owner's manual for "we the people." It is written in simple English. You may know much of what you will read on the following pages. My goal is to present the book in a fashion that will allow you to share it with your children.

Our children are our future. They will inherit this great nation in the not-too-distant future. They need to know the difference between a "Constitutional Republic" (what we are in the United States), and an "Unlimited Democracy" (what we are not).

If this book goes unread, it will not communicate anything. So, first, I want to share the case for reading this book – and for reading, period.

I agreed to speak to a seventh-grade school assembly on National Reading Day. For most who seek public office or serve in one, this is a "photo opportunity," or "photo op." They call this kind of appearance "earned media." It means free publicity you earn by doing something newsworthy.

If this is the way you view the invitation, what you say is really not important, as long as you talk about reading. You get your picture in the paper with a caption: "Congressman talks to students at Parkview School on National Reading Day."

I am not a politician by training. I didn't look at the invitation from a political standpoint. For me, this talk represented an opportunity to communicate something important to the kids. I agonized for three weeks about what I would say.

Seventh-graders are a tough audience. You have to capture their attention in the first couple of minutes. Grade-school children will typically sit in awe if they think you are an important visitor. A Rotary Club will sit quietly and tune you out if they aren't interested. But, if you don't have a seventh-grader's attention, it becomes obvious.

I began with the question: "By a show of hands, **how many of you have a personal computer**?" About half the students raised their hands.

"Wrong answer," I told them. "Every one of you should have raised your hand. **You all have a personal computer**. Your personal computer is located between your ears, and below your hairline.

"And your personal computer is better than any computer money can buy. I know – you want to know why. 'Why?' was my favorite question when I was in the seventh grade.

"So, why is your personal computer better than any computer money can buy? Because your personal computer can **think**, it can **dream**, it can **imagine**. Money can't buy a computer that can **think**, or **dream**, or **imagine**.

"God equipped your personal computer with software and an operating system. It was all preloaded. There are many ways for you to receive input, and create output.

"Orville and Wilbur Wright used their personal computers to **dream** about flying. They **imagined** what it would be like to fly. They **thought** about how they could do it.

"Walt Disney had a **dream**. Some people who work at Disney World and Epcot today are called **imagineers**. They **imagine** things and **think** up ways to make it happen.

"**America is a country of dreamers**.

"Dr. Martin Luther King made a famous speech called '**I Have a Dream**.' He read the Declaration of Independence and the U.S. Constitution. He read the Bible. He **dreamed** of an America that would finally reach its goal of treating all people equally.

"I **dreamed** of having my own bus company. I **imagined** what the buses would look like. I **thought** about how to do it. You or your family may have traveled on my dream to Epcot or Disney World, Washington, D.C., or just across town.

"'Alright,' you say, 'you still haven't told me why I have to read. You said I could get input from a lot of places. Why can't I just visit Epcot? Why can't I watch television? Why can't I watch movies? **Why do I have to read?'**

"Because when you go to Disney World and Epcot, **you are looking at Walt Disney's dream**. When you watch a movie, **you are watching someone else's imagination**. And, when you watch the 6 o'clock news, **you are watching what someone else thinks is news**.

"If you don't spend some of your time reading, you will spend the rest of your life *looking at other people's dreams; watching other people's imagination; and thinking what other people think*."

I gave this talk to seventh-graders, but don't think you are exempt because you are an adult. Spend some time reading with, and to, your children and grandchildren. Share this story with them. Reading is important, even for grownups.

INTRODUCTION

When you go to the voting booth, you are choosing a direction for our country. If you are going to take a road trip, you have to know where you want to go before you choose a route to get you there.

Dr. Steven Covey, in his book *Seven Habits of Highly Successful People*, wrote, **"always begin with the end in mind**."

Any professional driver will tell you if you spend too much time looking at the scenery, you are going to wind up somewhere you didn't plan. You better know where you are going and know what is behind you. You need to know what is to your right and what is to your left.

Some of what I have written in this book is about America from conception and birth, to the present day. Some is about possible highways to the future. And finally, some is about what I believe needs to be done in order to preserve our Republic.

This book is part autobiography, part genealogy, and part politics. It also has some philosophy and economics.

1

Keta

My wife said you would not read this book if it had nothing in it but politics. She said I have to tell some of "our" story. If I told our whole story, I wouldn't have any space left for the political stuff.

We have led unusual lives. We are descended from people who led unusual lives. For starters, Keta (Kē´-tah) and I married 19 days after we met. It wouldn't have taken that long if she hadn't lost her birth certificate. She spent about a week looking for it. We finally had to get a certified copy from Frankfort, Kentucky.

Forty-two years later, we are still married. That would be unusual even if we had a normal courtship.

My dad was married four times. My mother made three attempts at marriage. Keta's dad was married three times. Her mother was married twice. We did not have good role models on how to make a marriage work.

Both of our fathers died married. Both of our mothers live single. You would need a program to determine the players at a family reunion. We come from what they politely call "blended families." At the time of our marriage, we called them "broken homes." Keta tells people, "It's a miracle we are still married."

Our lives took a lot of twists and turns before our paths, and lives, merged on November 24, 1967. A full accounting will have to wait for the next book. What follows are a few highlights.

January nights are very cold in Appalachia. This part of America has places with names like Crane Creek, Red Bird, Squabble Creek and Possum Trot. "Hollers" (small, sheltered valleys) are populated by lifeless cars and pick-up trucks, with weeds and saplings as silent occupants. Vehicles that move wear a common coat of clay and dust.

Many mountain people use newspaper for both insulation and wallpaper. The clear plastic "storm windows" nailed to the window frames move in and out with the wind. One side of an occupant cooks and the other side freezes, depending upon their position to the pot bellied stove.

It is into this world that my wife was born in 1949. It could have been May 3 or May 5, take your pick. Her mommy says it was the former, the State of Kentucky says it was the latter. They agree that she was born in Manchester, Kentucky, the Clay County seat. She is the second child born to the former Sylvia Baker and Mark Dean.

She began life not far from the Clay County courthouse lawn. This is where her great-grandfather, "Bad" Tom Baker, met his maker. His picture graces the back cover of the book *Days of Darkness*. It was taken just minutes before he was gunned down from a building across the street. Such was life, or death, during the "feuds" in the mountains of Kentucky.

A member of the Kentucky militia guards "Bad" Tom Baker.

Keta (nicknamed "Skeeter"), spent her early years there with her older sister Phyllis (nicknamed "Blackie"), and younger sister Lou (nicknamed "NaNa"). Nicknames are standard equipment in the country. Their younger brother Mark became deaf from high fever at 10 months of age. He began boarding at the Kentucky School for the Deaf at Danville, Kentucky while in kindergarten.

When Keta was old enough, she walked to school and back with her sisters "'cross the swingin' bridge" over the South Fork. The framed, weathered floor boards, hanging from the twin cables, banged underfoot. They had to step over the occasional space created by a missing board. From time to time, this stream would be an unwelcome visitor to the family restaurant.

Keta, age 3 (above); sister Phyllis and Dr. Keta (right).

The Oneida Baptist Institute is situated on the highest point in town. When high water from the South Fork threatened, the girls stayed in the dorms with the "campus kids." Keta's parents and the other adults would scramble to save what they could from the rising floodwaters. After the salvage and clean up, they would move back to "town."

Phyllis and Keta (with Pepsi). Right: The "swingin' bridge" over the South Fork.

The girls ran barefoot through the town and surrounding hills. They helped Sylvia, their mother, when she could catch 'em. They would hoe the garden and pick corn and beans, while wearing "hand-me-downs." They stood on boxes to reach the sink and stove. They waited on customers. Many customers were miners with white circles around their eyes on otherwise coal-black-ened faces.

The Dean family kitchen and living area was Dean's Café. Above the café and below the tin roof was the family sleeping area. It was hot in the summer and cold in the winter. The café opened at 7 a.m., unless some impatient customer yelled from the porch – "SYLL-V-YA ... WHEN YA GONNA OPEN UP?"

Seven days a week, the café would close when the Dean family went to bed. The only private life they had was taking baths and sleeping upstairs. Most people paid for their meals; some couldn't. They didn't turn anyone away hungry. They got what they needed "on account." Many ledger entries remain "unpaid" to this day.

Keta in fourth grade.

A porch ran the length of the building, from Dean's Café to Dean's Pool Hall. The porch had a "liar's bench," and a normally adequate supply of chairs. When the seating capacity was exceeded, kids sat on the floor of the porch, feet dangling above the dusty street. No women or girls were allowed in the pool hall, except the owners' daughters.

The café was connected to the pool hall by an inside hallway and storage area as well. This storage area was where 5-year-old Phyllis, 4-year-old Keta and 2½-year-old Lou patiently sat on straw-lined wooden crates, trying to hatch Banty Chicken eggs. From time to time, the men passing through asked, with a straight face, "We got any chickens yet?" The egg man had convinced the three little girls that they could hatch the eggs if they sat on 'em long enough.

A lot of cussin' and some drinkin' went on in the pool hall, along with an occasional shootin'. Clay County is a "dry" county. This doesn't mean that locals don't drink. It means you can't sell liquor legally. They occasionally vote on whether or not to make the county "wet." The bootleggers put up the money, the churches provide the ground troops, and each time the measure is on the ballot, it is defeated. Politics does make strange bedfellows, even in the mountains.

Law enforcement remains slow coming to Clay County. Keta's dad packed a .32 caliber Smith & Wesson revolver often referred to as an "owl head." It was a hammerless, short-barrel, five-shot model. The five-round cylinder didn't make as big a bulge in his hip pocket. The hammerless design didn't snag on his pocket when he needed it.

You couldn't set a washtub between the pool hall and the Pentecostal Holiness Church next door. Services were held on Sunday and four nights a week. Worship was a team sport, the pastor was simply the coach. They handled snakes a couple of times a year. Like Dean's Café and Pool Hall, service was over when folks went home.

When Keta was less than 18 months old, she took off all her clothes, and then decided to attend the evening church services. Someone brought word to Sylvia that Skeeter was running around the pulpit and through the pews in the buff. Worse yet, she was crawling up in parishioners' laps. Sylvia was too embarrassed to go get her, so she sent Keta's half-sister Jeanette to fetch the child nudist from church.

Most kids believe that normal is whatever they experience and wherever they live growing up. But Keta never felt her life was normal. Even the virtually unlimited supply of Pepsi, Big Red, Moon Pies and ice cream didn't help. Even plenty of change for the jukebox didn't shake the feeling she should be somewhere else.

If she thought life wasn't quite normal before a cold January night in 1963, it was getting ready to become less normal. It was a slow night in the café , and Keta and Phyllis were watching "Bonanza" on the black-and-white TV. Lou was upstairs. Runt and Toodles were two older boys who helped out in the pool hall. It was slow there, too, so they joined the Dean girls watching television. When the commotion broke out upstairs, Runt and Toodles headed for the hills. Keta headed for the stairs.

On her way up, Keta ran into her mother, half running and half falling down the stairs. Sylvia yelled, "Tell your sisters … we're leavin'." At Sylvia's direction, Phyllis jumped up on the counter and grabbed the cash box. She didn't know if her mommy wanted the cash or the other pistol they kept there. Her daddy didn't know either – he grabbed the box from Phyllis.

Sylvia and the girls bolted out of the café. They ran through the snow-covered remnants of the summer garden. A neighbor took them in until their dad left the next morning. Dad was gone, and they needed a car. The only one handy was a '55 Olds, a baby blue and white coupe. Mark, their daddy, had won it in a recent poker game. He had the keys in his pocket.

Sylvia went looking for "Youngin." Youngin wasn't so young. When he was sober, he worked part-time at Brown's Garage. Youngin was worried that Mark would find out he helped them. Sylvia convinced him she was leaving town and Mark wouldn't know.

A coat hanger and two minutes later, Youngin had the doors unlocked. Sylvia and the girls loaded the car. Once loaded, Youngin hot-wired the ignition and they were off. They arrived at Granny Baker's in Jeffersonville, Indiana, with Lou riding in the back seat. She was lying with her shabby stray dog on the stuff that wouldn't fit in the trunk.

It was the end of Keta's mother's first marriage, her dad's second. Keta didn't know it yet, but her parents' divorce had set her on the path to meet her future husband. Life

Keta's Jeffersonville High School senior piciture.

wouldn't be easy living in Granny Baker's basement. Sylvia had a hard time finding work. Mark didn't pay child support. The girls had to find work. First they did babysitting and household work; later they found real jobs.

A neighborhood lady, Marie Robertson, took them under her wing. She took Sylvia out to apply for jobs and gave them groceries when she could. As a former nurse, she was their health care, using over-the-counter remedies. More than 45 years later, Keta still considers Marie her best friend.

"If she thought life wasn't quite normal
before a cold January night in 1963,
it was getting ready to become less nomal."

2

Mike

It was a balmy night in St. Petersburg, Florida, in January 1963. While Keta and her family were headed for Jeffersonville, Indiana, I was boarding a plane for Louisville, Kentucky. Final destination: New Albany, Indiana. I didn't know it yet, but I was on a path to meet my future wife. By the end of January 1963, we were less than five miles apart as the crow flies, but it will take more than four years to close that gap.

My first job was working as a "bag boy" for Publix Supermarket in St. Petersburg for a dollar an hour. I worked 24 hours a week while attending Dixie Hollins High School. This was my first experience with taxes. I grossed $24 a week and my "take home" pay was $18.54. I put the check in the bank, and kept the tips for spending money.

I was born December 17, 1945, in Louisville, Kentucky. I was the only child of the former Nora Vermillion and Robert E. "Bob" Sodrel. At the time, Mom and Dad were living in the government housing projects off of Beechwood Avenue in New Albany. Mom says that when they brought me home from the hospital nursery, I slept in a dresser drawer. They didn't have a crib.

Wainwright Court, in the Beechwood government housing project, was my home until my parents divorced. It was the end of Mom's first marriage, Dad's third. Unlike Keta, I don't remember the divorce. My earliest memory is riding in a bicycle basket. By this time, Mom had remarried and my stepdad, Ed Keller, was attending the pharmacy school at Purdue University in West Lafayette, Indiana.

It was cold, and I was wearing an aviator cap. I was stuffed in a dirty-clothes bag with just my head sticking out. Ed and I were on our way to do the laundry. After Ed graduated, he took a job in Champaign, Illinois. When Keta was brought home to live over Dean's Café in Oneida, Kentucky, I was living over a drug store in Champaign, Illinois.

Mike and his dad Bob on Wainwright Court in the Beechwood "projects" (before they were bricked).

Divorce is confusing for little people. For many years I would call Ed "Dad," and call Dad "Bob." I guess that's normal. I saw more of Ed than Dad in my early years. My youth was more like a play than a movie. It was different acts, on different sets, kind of loosely connected. They say the family should give children "roots and wings." I grew up short on roots and long on wings.

By the time I started first grade, we were back in New Albany, Indiana. Before I graduated from New Albany High School, I changed schools eight times. I changed my residence more often than that – summer here, winter there, Christmas break spent wherever I

Third birthday at "Pap's" on Corydon Pike in New Albany. (Note the clothes line in the kitchen.)

wasn't going to school. It was like living life as a perpetual tourist.

By January 1963, Dad was married for the fourth time. My stepmother Donna had two daughters by a previous marriage, Toni and Chris. My half-sister Patsy was Dad's daughter by his second wife. My half-brothers and half-sister – Rick, Steve, Kevin and Debra Keller – were born between Purdue University and St. Petersburg. Mom and Ed were not divorced yet. My other half-brother Billy Wasserman came along later. When you grow up this way, life is a big grey area. Not much is absolute.

I had a senior English teacher at Dixie Hollins High School in St. Petersburg that lived in a black-and-white world. She didn't see any grey. The semester term paper was 50 percent of your grade. It had to be submitted by a certain time and date, no exceptions. I missed the deadline. I made my best effort to negotiate a 72-hour extension. She wouldn't concede that, in the infinite time and space of the universe, 72 hours more or less on a term paper didn't really matter. She was unmoved. She said, "You will have to go to summer school." I told her, "No, I will have to go back to Indiana. They only require three years of English to graduate."

I told Mom I was going back to Indiana to finish high school. I am not sure I gave a reason, or if she asked for one. She called Dad to tell him I wouldn't be coming for Christmas break. She told him I would come up after the break to finish school in Indiana. We made the reservation on Eastern Airlines. I told her I would call and make arrangements to get picked up at the Louisville airport.

I had attended New Albany High School my sophomore year. I really wasn't looking forward to living with Dad and Donna. I cashed out my checking account, packed my things and called my cousin Terry Sodrel to pick me up on arrival. He had an apartment in New Albany. He was 21 years old and was going to Indiana University Southeast while driving a truck part time for the family trucking company.

Sellersburg Elementary, fourth grade.

I settled in with Terry, enrolled in school, paid my book rentals and student fees, life was good ... until the latter part of January. Dad called Mom. He said,

"I thought Mike was coming up to finish school." She said, "We put him on a plane a couple of weeks ago." Whoops! He called Terry for another short conversation.

"Have you seen Mike?" he asked.

Terry answered, "Yeah, he's here."

When I came to the phone Dad said he would pick me up in 30 minutes. I responded that I was comfortable where I was. I told him that I had paid my fees, enrolled in school, and was attending classes regularly.

His response went something like, "Either your *** is moving up here on the hill, or you are going back to Florida."

Mike's senior picture.

I was thinking, "Hmm, Florida isn't an option." So I said, "Since you put it that way, Pop, I'll be ready in 30 minutes."

I think he was holding onto a grudge from Christmas of '58. Eastern Airlines had been on strike. He called Greyhound to find an express bus to Florida. He put me and three suitcases on the Express Greyhound Bus. He called Mom and gave her the arrival time in St. Pete and the unit number of the bus. It came in right on time, 22 hours later. But I wasn't on it.

I had decided to go sightseeing in Chattanooga, Atlanta and Tallahassee. Two suitcases of Christmas presents and one of personal effects were parked in lockers at the bus stations, while I went out to see what I could see. I slept between the stops.

Greyhound had issued three original tickets and a ticket stub for an express bus trip to St. Pete. I used the first ticket to board at Louisville. I used the second ticket to board at Chattanooga. I used the third ticket to board at Atlanta. It wasn't hard. They were swamped with passengers. An "extra section" was rolling out every hour or so, going south. As long as you had a ticket going in the direction of your destination, you were good to go.

I realized at Tallahassee that I didn't have a ticket for St. Pete. All I had was a stub. I watched the system. The drivers would get on the bus, collect the tickets, and then push the door closed to check out with the dispatcher. I had a Red Cap put my bags under a bus bound for St. Pete and waited. When the driver went to check out, I opened the door and took a seat.

The driver returned to the bus and made his last head count. He counted again. He announced that everyone on board would have to produce their ticket stubs. I showed my ticket stub. He looked at his paperwork again, shrugged, and pulled out. About an hour south of Tallahassee I went to the front of the bus.

I told the driver, "I have a confession to make."

He responded, "You're the one without a ticket." He kept on rollin'.

When I stepped off the bus in St. Pete, Mom exclaimed, "Mike! If you weren't on this particular bus, your Dad was leaving Louisville and checking every bus station between here and there."   I breathed a sigh of relief. He had almost five months to cool off. I guess somewhere in the subconscious of the barely 13-year-old mind, not showing up on time is your way of seeing if anyone notices you. Or, maybe it is your way of punishing your parents for the way you are living. I just remember being relieved that I showed up before he started south.

Before Keta and I met, cousin Terry and I headed out west and picked up Route 66 at St. Louis. Forty-six hours later we were in Huntington Beach, California. It didn't take long to figure out that two guys with flat tops and a farmer's tan didn't fit in very well in the Golden State. Maybe it was the Indiana tags on the '62 Impala Super Sport. We returned home in just 42 hours.

Before Keta and I married, I was a bank messenger, I drove a truck, I worked on an assembly line, I was a mechanic, I enrolled in and left college, I got engaged and disengaged. I completed Army Basic Training and AIT at Ft. Leonard Wood, Missouri, and went looking for *something* in half of the 50 states. I would find it less than five miles away.

At Ft. Leonard Wood.

But, in 1963, all this was in the future. I climbed the stairs to the Eastern Airlines Constellation. I found my window seat just slightly behind the props. With an increasing whine, the propeller on the Wright 3350 outside my window slowly turned. The 18 supercharged cylinders had three exhaust pipes with six cylinders feeding each pipe. They belched black and blue smoke as the engine coughed and sprang to life.

I was always amazed to watch the red and yellow engine exhaust on take off. It would finally turn blue* as the "Connie's" engines were leaned out at cruising altitude. (To see, Google "Lockheed Constellation" on YouTube.) I usually flew "night flight" on the plane that carried the mail. It was cheaper.

Three hours and 30 minutes at 18,000 feet, and we made our final approach to Standiford Field in Louisville. When I stepped out onto the platform of the stairs upon arrival, two things were immediately evident. It was a cold January in Kentucky in 1963, and I didn't bring a coat.

3
Mike and Keta

Fast forward to November 5, 1967. A friend walked into Frisch's Drive-In Restaurant where I sat munching a double-deck hamburger. John said he had a date, would I loan him my Camaro? He would leave his motorcycle for me. Sure, I said, and we exchanged keys.

I was still hanging around Frisch's when my friend returned with his date. He backed into one of the spaces around back. I walked out and took a seat in the passenger bucket seat. Keta sat on the console. Someone wanted to race. John asked if I minded.

While John was busy abusing my four-speed Muncie gearbox, I was busy talking with the future Mrs. Sodrel. She told me she was going to a dance at Ewing Lane the next night. If the band wasn't good, she would be home at 10 o'clock.

I was there waiting in the parking lot of her mother's apartment at 10. I asked her to marry me on our first date; she was 18, I was 21. She said, "You're crazy. I don't even know you." Nineteen days later we married. It wouldn't have taken that long if she hadn't lost her birth certificate.

November 24, 1967: She and I took a lap around Frisch's looking for a couple of witnesses. We had obtained a certified copy of her birth certificate, taken the required blood tests, and been issued a marriage license. Frank Lind (now deceased) and Larry Kelley agreed to "stand up" for us.

In a civil ceremony, performed by Justice of the Peace Mike Marra in Jeffersonville, we were pronounced man and wife. At this point, Keta had not met either of my parents, and I had not met her father. Such is life in a blended family. A one-night honeymoon in a local hotel, and we embarked on what is now more than 42 years of marriage.

When we married, I had a negative net worth of about $3,000. The '67 Camaro was my only asset, and I owed more on it than it was worth. We spent the first winter in a cottage on the banks of the Ohio River. Neither of us was working. We were out of propane gas for the furnace with no prospects of getting any. After cashing in Coke bottles and taking the back seat out of the car looking for loose change, BankAmericard (now Visa) was kind enough to send an unsolicited credit card.

Mike and Keta early years.

The credit card kept the cat, the dog, the raccoon and the newlyweds fed for the winter. My net worth was declining. Ironically, when I went to work in the spring, I was collecting delinquent accounts for BankAmericard at Citizens Fidelity Bank. Keta went to work at Sears Roebuck and Co.

We eventually moved to the bottom of an old house on East 16th, south of Main Street, in New Albany. Keta was now pregnant with our first-born. I sold the Camaro to get ready to support the baby. For two months we rode the Daisy Line Bus to work while I scraped together a down payment on a VW Beetle.

Mike and pregnant Keta in front of their VW Beetle.

In another bit of irony, seven years later I bought the Daisy Line and Home Transit Bus Companies. They would become The Free Enterprise System, Inc.

I returned to driving a truck full-time in early '69. Keta delivered Noah on December 11 of that year. Blue Cross/Blue Shield refused to pay for the two false labors and the delivery. Noah was born 269 days after I changed jobs and the policy went into effect. The waiting period was 270 days. I had to pay the hospital for the delivery. It was almost $1,000. At the time, a new VW Beetle was selling for $2,000.

When we brought Noah home from the hospital, the rats were attracted to the baby formula. I tried to convince Keta they were mice. That worked until a long tail was hanging out of the kitchen trash can. I came home from making a truck run to find a note: "Gone to Mommy's. I will come back when you find a better place to live. Love, Keta."

In the mid-1970s, I worked for the family trucking business, Sodrel Truck lines, Inc. The Sodrel family has been in the transportation business in Southern Indiana for almost 150 years.

My great-grandfather Martin Sodrel settled on a farm in the Ohio River Bottoms below Derby (downriver) in Perry County, Indiana. His farm was under the hill (at the foot of the hill). His first vocation was farmer.

After the Civil War, he realized that his farm products were worth more in New Orleans than they were in Southern Indiana. So he took up flatboating to increase his income. He would load the flatboat with farm products, and float down the Ohio and Mississippi Rivers to New Orleans. After selling all the products off the flatboat, he would take the boat apart and sell it for lumber. Then he would walk back to Indiana.

At the time the lower Mississippi River was infested with river pirates. Martin's obituary after his death in July 1919 noted, "He was one of the best pilots to ever ply the Mississippi. He never lost a boat or a cargo all the years he was in the trade." He read the river well, and he was a crack shot with a rifle or a shotgun.

My grandfather Noah F. "Pap" Sodrel ran a ferry service from Southern Indiana to Kentucky on a home-made johnboat. He delivered mail in Perry County on horseback shortly after the turn of the 20th century. In 1929, he bought his first truck.

"Pap" Sodrel in the middle with Browning shotgun in the crook of his arm.

My dad Robert E. "Bob" Sodrel and his brothers Ernest and Noah A. "Jack" Sodrel began trucking on their own in the 1930s. In the early 1950s, they all pooled their resources and efforts, first as a partnership, and then as a corporation.

The family tree had grown pretty large by the 1970s with the founders' children and spouses of children. I decided I wanted my own company. I didn't want to move, and I didn't want to compete with the family trucking business.

The Daisy Line and Home Transit were two local transit bus companies that were in serious trouble. I bought three 1949 GMC transit buses, and merged the two transit bus operations under a new corporation, The Free Enterprise System, Inc. We still have the original three buses.

I named the new company Free Enterprise because we refused to accept federal, state or local government subsidies. We operated the transit operation in Southern Indiana, and between Southern Indiana and Louisville on just fare box receipts – our only operating revenue was the 60-cent fares dropped in the fare box as the passengers boarded our buses.

We operated the transit lines from June 1976 until February 1983 without any government assistance. We transferred the scheduled transit operation to the Transit Authority of River City (TARC) in 1983 and continued to grow our charter bus service.

In 1987, I purchased Sodrel Truck Lines, Inc. from the remaining family members. We later added Sodrel Logistics and The Star of America. Sodrel Logistics (SOLO) operates small trucks in retail delivery, and Star is a charter bus company.

When I was elected to Congress, I was required to resign as an officer, director or employee of any of the family firms. Our son, Noah, leads the group of companies today.

Indiana Mike and Keta.

So what does all this have to do with politics? When you are reading something, you need to know who wrote it. I am not an academic, writing about a theoretical world. I am not a politician, writing about a political world. I used to tell my colleagues in Congress, "Washington, D.C., is 64 square miles surrounded by reality." I have spent my life in reality.

Neither Keta nor I had a "Leave it to Beaver" upbringing. We faced the reality of broken homes when divorce wasn't cool. We faced the reality of medical bills insurance wouldn't cover. We faced the reality of balancing a family budget. We faced the reality of not being able to afford a car. I do not write this as part of the political, academic or economic elite of America.

I am just an American citizen that took the time to read what the Founders of the American republic wrote, and I read much of what they read. I am self-educated in the classics, including: Adam Smith's *Wealth of Nations*, 1776; John Locke's *Two Treaties on Government*, 1690; Thomas Paine's *Common Sense* and *Rights of Man*. I read the Declaration of Independence and the U.S. Constitution and *The Federalist Papers* written by Hamilton, Madison and Jay.

I want to make our system of government, as well as the competing styles of government, understandable for people who don't have the time to read volumes on the subject of liberty. I want to make our economic system understandable. Politics is important, but politics is just a vehicle. You need to consider your destination.

To our Founders, liberty was the most important issue. To quote Patrick Henry, "I know not what course others may take ... but for me, **give me liberty or give me death**." Maybe liberty is not important to a majority of Americans anymore. I pray not. Maybe a majority of us are content to be herded around by a government shepherd.

Or, maybe the majority just can't see the forest for the trees. They go from issue to issue without really understanding the long-term consequences of short-term actions. I hope this book will help you decide. A house divided against itself cannot stand.

Mike and Keta today.

4

The Political Right is on the Left, and the Center is on the Right

Almost any news source uses the terms political left, right, and the term center, or centrist. If I gave you a pen and paper, and asked you to draw a political graph showing the political left, right and center, it would probably look like this:

Figure 1

This seems logical. The political left is on the left, the right is on the right, and the political center is in the middle. It seems logical, but who said politics is logical?

When someone speaks of the far political left, there is general agreement that they are talking about a Communist, or communism. Similarly, if they are speaking about the far political right, it refers to a Fascist, or fascism.

Actually, there isn't much difference between communism and fascism. The **Communist** believes government should **own** all the nation's assets (property and resources). The **Fascist** believes government should **control** all of the nation's assets; government ownership is optional.

In some respects, **control** is better than **owner-ship**. If I gave you a choice of two cars: One car will be given to you outright with a clear title – it is your car. **You own it**. But I can tell you **when** you can drive it, **where** you can drive it, and **who** you can take with you. Or you can choose the other car. It is a leased car that you will never own. But you can drive it when you want to, where you want to, and take along whoever you want to. You would probably choose the leased car. After all, **what good is ownership if you have no control**?

Since ownership and control are so close to being the same thing, the far left Communist and the far right Fascist aren't really far apart. **Communist/ownership** and **Fascist/control** are very close in concept. So, we will bend the ends of our straight line graph from this straight line:

Figure 1

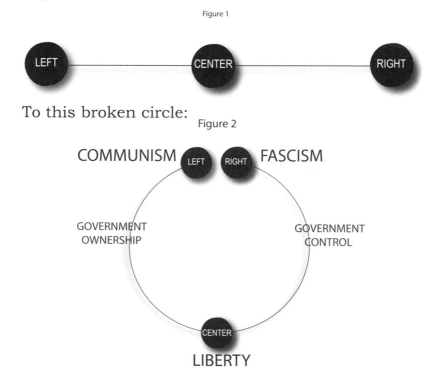

To this broken circle:

Figure 2

We bent the ends of our straight line graph up until they almost touched. Now we have to make another adjustment in our graph.

Basically, the new left doesn't really care if government **owns** the nation's assets, or if government **controls** them. As long as government grows in size and influence, they will take whatever they can get. So our graph needs to be shifted 90 degrees to the left.

It goes from this: Figure 2

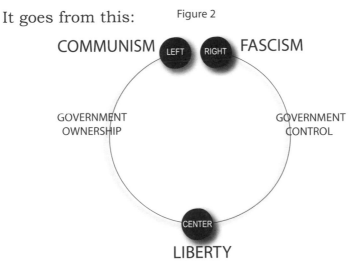

To this: Figure 3

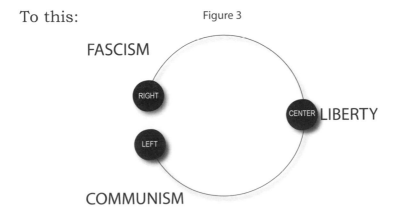

The new left is made up of the Communist, the Socialist, the Fascist, modern liberals, progressives, the religious left and their fellow travelers (people who go along with them).

The new right is made up of the conservatives, the Christian right, Libertarians, constitutionalists and capitalists.

If we take our broken circle and draw a line down the center, we now have the new political left and new right. It looks like this:

Figure 4

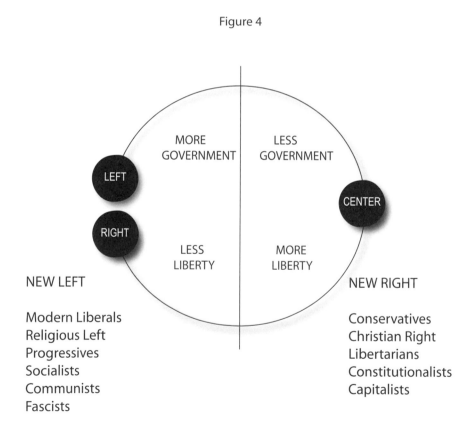

NEW LEFT

Modern Liberals
Religious Left
Progressives
Socialists
Communists
Fascists

NEW RIGHT

Conservatives
Christian Right
Libertarians
Constitutionalists
Capitalists

Those who are on the new left favor higher taxes, a bigger government and less individual liberty. They are basically in favor of more **government ownership** or **government control** of our nation's property and resources.

Those who are on the new right favor stable or lower taxes, a smaller government and more individual liberty. They are basically in favor of **individual ownership** or **individual control** of our nation's property and resources.

Tune in to C-SPAN and listen to the floor debates in Congress. With few exceptions, the debates are about **ownership** or **control**.

Who has **control** over the money you earn? **You**, or **your government**? Who has **control** over the property you own? **You**, or **the government**? Who takes **control** of your worldly possessions when you die? **Your heirs**, or **the government**?

To me, liberty is where America came in. Individual liberty is what the Founders were trying to achieve. The U.S. Constitution was designed to protect our God-granted natural rights, as well as individual liberty. Any movement toward more government control or government ownership takes us away from liberty.

"Basically the new left doesn't really care if government owns the nations assets, or if government controls them. As long as government grows in size and influence, they will take whatever they can get."

5

The Political Left Needs to Buy a Dictionary – or Use One

Words do have meaning. In order to communicate with each other, **words must have meaning**. Part of our problem is that liberals and conservatives do not speak the same language. The words **sound** the same when they are spoken, but they don't **mean** the same thing when they are heard.

Take the word **tolerant**. Dictionary definition: tol/er/ant (täl' er ent) *adj.* 1. Willing to let other people do as they think best; **willing to endure beliefs and actions of which one does not approve**: *A free nation is tolerant towards all religious beliefs.* 2. Able to endure or resist the action of a drug, poison, or other, usually harmful substance.

When a liberal uses the word tolerant, they really mean "to approve of, or to promote." **I can and do tolerate a lot of things I do not approve of and things I certainly will not promote**. The fact that I do not celebrate "alternative lifestyles" does not mean I am intolerant of them.

All of the words I have used in this book are used in the actual dictionary definition. I will also try to avoid any **nuances**: nu/ance (nōō' äns') *n.* 1. **A subtle distinction or variation**. My writing style will be straightforward: proceeding in a straight course or manner; direct, undeviating; outspoken, candid; clear-cut, precise.

I spent years trying to understand the nuanced difference between communism and fascism. Joseph Stalin's old Soviet Union was called the **U.S.S.R.**: The **U**nited **S**oviet **S**ocialist **R**epublics. Adolph Hitler's Nazi Party was called the National **Socialist** German Workers Party (NSDAP).

Stalin's **communist** government killed over 20 million of his countrymen. Hitler's **fascist** government deliberately killed more than six million Jews and millions of other European civilians.

Both governments called themselves **socialist institutions**, and both killed or imprisoned millions of people who disagreed with them. So what is the "nuanced" difference? The basic difference between **communism** and **fascism** is the difference between **ownership** and **control**.

A Communist believes government should **own** all of a country's assets. "In this sense, the theory of the Communists may be summed up in the single phrase: **Abolition of private property**." – Taken from *The Communist Manifesto* written in 1848 by Karl Marx and Friedrich Engels.

A Fascist believes government should **control** all of a country's assets. The Fascist is willing for individuals to own businesses, factories, farms, etc. However, they must use these assets to achieve the goals of the government.

Both forms of government are very oppressive. Anyone who doesn't toe the government line is crushed, imprisoned, or just eliminated. The media and educational system are government owned, or government controlled. In both systems, the individual exists to serve the state.

It is sometimes equally difficult to tell the difference between a **Socialist** and a **Communist**. The Socialist and the Communist have the same goal in mind; they just use different means to get there.

The Communist believes armed revolution is the only practical way to install Communism. "The Communists disdain to conceal their views and aims. They openly declare that their ends can be attained only by the **forcible overthrow** of all existing social conditions." – *The Communist Manifesto*.

The Socialist believes the same thing can be accomplished through legislation and elections. "It therefore aims at the establishment of a society in which ... **the economic power of individuals and classes (shall be) abolished** through the **collective ownership** and democratic control of the economic resources of the community. **It seeks to secure these ends by the methods of political democracy**." (The Fabian Society, 1938)

So the difference between a **Communist** and a **Fascist** is the difference between **ownership** and **control**. The difference between a **Communist** and a **Socialist** is the difference between **bullets** and **ballots**.

The communist will take your property with bullets. The socialist will take your property with ballots and call it social justice.

In our hemisphere, Fidel Castro and Hugo Chavez are good examples. They are close allies with common beliefs and goals. Fidel Castro came to power in Cuba with **bullets**. Hugo Chavez came to power in Venezuela with **ballots**.

Anyone who believes the acquisition of General Motors by the United States government is not a Socialist transaction does not understand the term. The Communist would have taken GM by force; the Socialist took it with legislation.

We will leave this chapter with definitions taken from my Thorndike-Barnhart Dictionary.

Fascism (fash' iz'em) *n.* 1. Any system of government in which **property is privately owned**. But all industry and labor are regulated by a strong national government, **while all opposition is rigorously suppressed**: A basic idea of fascism was: **Everyone shall work, but no one shall work against the state** (Emory S. Bogardus*). 2. The doctrines, principles or methods of such a government or of a political party favoring such a government. 3. Any movement favoring such a government.

Here is a slightly shortened definition of **communism** (kom' yu niz'em) *n.* 1. A system in which most or **all property is owned by the state** and is supposed to be shared by all. Communism comes from a philosophy based on the writings of Karl Marx and Friedrich Engels

---

* Emory S. Borgardus (1882-1973) founded one of the first sociology departments at an American University in 1915 at USC (University Southern California). – Wikipedia

Definitions for Communism, Fascism, Socialism, etc. taken from Thorndike-Barnhart Dictionary prepared in cooperation with World Book, Inc. Copyright 1939.

in the 1800s and seeks the overthrow of non-communist societies in behalf of the laboring class, usually as the result of a series of struggles of class conflict. 2. A political, social and economic system in which the state, governed by an elite party, controls production, labor and distribution, and largely, the social and cultural life and thought of the people. 3. A social order in which property is held in common by the community or the state; communalism.

The definition included a short contrast between **communism** and **socialism**, which I include here: "communism and socialism are systems of social organization under which the means of production and distribution of goods are **transferred from private hands to the government**. The classic difference between the two systems lies in **the different means they take to establish themselves**: Communism emphasizes the impracticability of replacing the existing social order by any means other than **armed force or outside intervention**; the advocates of **socialism** seek to establish it by peaceful means, **through election and legislation** rather than force. The practical differences between the two systems are sometimes varied and great."

General Motors did not become **Government** Motors by an armed takeover. The **socialist takeover** of GM was through legislation. It was, by definition, a **transfer from private hands to the government** of the **means of production** of the largest American car maker. It doesn't get more socialist than that.

"So the difference between a **Communist** and a **Fascist** is the difference between **Ownership** and **Control**. The Difference between a **Communist** and a **Socialist** is the difference between **Bullets** and **Ballots**."

6

The Majority Does Not Rule In America, the Constitution Does

You do not live in a democracy. The United States of America is a **constitutional republic**, not an unlimited democracy. In America, the majority **does not rule – the law does**.

Our Founders were tired of **snob rule**. They did not want to be ruled by kings and queens and other royalty anymore. On the other hand, they didn't trust **mob rule**. In fact, they did not want to be ruled by people at all.

So they chose to be **ruled by the law**. Thomas Jefferson made this clear when he said: "In questions of power then, let no more be heard of confidence in man, but bind him down from mischief by the chains of the Constitution."

When you recite the Pledge of Allegiance to our flag, you say, "... and to the **Republic** for which it stands." It is the Statue of **Liberty** that stands in New York harbor, not the Goddess of Democracy. We are a **constitutional republic** with democratically elected officials.

Patrick Henry was a Virginian. He was an American revolutionary, a patriot and a legislator. On the eve of America's war for independence, in March 1775, he delivered a passionate speech that ended with this line: "I know not what course others may take; but as for me, give me **liberty** or give me death." He did not say, "Give me **democracy** or give me death."

The New Hampshire flag still says, "LIVE FREE OR DIE." We inherited this nation from people who **valued their liberty more than life itself**. Our Founders believed that people were "endowed by their **creator** with certain unalienable rights."

A short comparison between the English Democracy and the American Republic is in order. In England, at a place called Runnymeade in the year 1215, a group of nobles put the sword to King John's throat and said in effect, "King, we want some of your power. Here, sign this." The king signed the Magna Carta, and the foundation for the English democracy was laid.

In 1776, a group of Americans told King George in effect, "Thank you very much King, we don't need any of your power." When Thomas Jefferson penned our Declaration of Independence, he made it clear our rights came directly to us from "**nature and nature's God**" when he wrote that people were "endowed by their **Creator** with certain unalienable rights." Our rights were not granted by the king or any government.

He went on to say that "to **secure** these rights, governments are instituted among men." In other words, our government does not exist to **issue or grant** rights. Our government exists to **secure or protect** our God-granted rights.

The first 10 amendments to the United States Constitution are commonly called "The Bill of Rights." The Bill of Rights **does not** give you any rights. The Bill of Rights was designed to keep government from taking away your God-granted rights. It even says so.

The Ninth Amendment basically says, "Our failure to mention a right here doesn't mean the people don't have it." The Tenth Amendment states in effect: "The federal government only has the power granted to it by the U.S. Constitution. All other power is retained by the individual states, or the people."

So, in the American republic, **the people granted certain rights to their government**. In the English democracy, **the government granted certain rights to the people**.

Because the English king's power was unlimited, the English government's power was unlimited. The American people never granted unlimited power to their government. The U.S. Constitution and state constitutions were designed to **limit government power**.

If you wanted to be an English knight centuries ago, you had to swear an oath to protect and defend your king, with your life if necessary. If you want to serve as an American knight (i.e., soldier, sailor, marine or airman) you must swear an oath to protect and defend **the Constitution of the United States**. This is the difference between rule of people and rule of law. Our earthly king is not a person, it is the Constitution.

Very often someone in the media will use the term "Rule of Law." I have never heard one of them explain what that means or explain the alternatives.

For centuries people were governed by **one** person **or a group** of people. It could have been a king, queen, pharaoh, emperor, empress or other title for rule by one person. Or, it could have been the "majority rule" of the ancient Greeks. Our Founders studied all of them.

The *Federalist Papers* were written to "sell" the newly crafted United States Constitution to the American people. These essays were written by James Madison, Alexander Hamilton and John Jay between October 1787 and May 1788. They wrote them over the pen name "Publius."

James Madison was our fourth President. He is usually credited with writing the United States Constitution. He writes in Federalist No. 10, "Hence it is that such democracies have ever been spectacles of turbulence and contention; have ever been found incompatible with personal security of the rights of property; and have in general been as short in their lives as they have been violent in their deaths."

When I teach school children about the "rule of law" I use a Western movie. I tell them I remember watching this movie about the Old West. In one scene the townspeople had decided to lynch (hang) a prisoner held in the local jail. The majority of the people in this town marched down to the jail to hang a prisoner.

I remember feeling sorry for the sheriff. He was all by himself. He stood on the porch of the jail with his Colt .45 and his double-barreled shotgun. He told the crowd they could not have the prisoner, and that the accused man would get a fair trial. In this case, the mob represented the **majority**, the sheriff represented the **Constitution**.

We will address some related subjects later. For example: What does "legislating from the bench" mean? Who can change the Constitution? The English Parliament can change the English Constitution. The U.S. Congress **cannot** change the U.S. Constitution. So who can? More later...

7
You're a What? Why?

By now you have learned that **communism** is about government **ownership** of a nation's assets. **Fascism** is about government **control** of a nation's assets.

You know by now that communism and socialism are virtually the same system. **Communism** is installed with **bullets**, and **socialism** comes to power with **ballots**. The goal of Communists and Socialists is to **eliminate private property**.

You know that **America is a Constitutional Republic**, not an **unlimited democracy**. The English government gave **limited rights to English citizens** at Runnymeade, England, in 1215. The **American citizens gave limited rights to their government** in 1787 at Philadelphia, Pennsylvania.

So, before we move to the right, let's discuss liberals, progressives and the religious left. I have dedicated a later chapter to the religious left and church-and-state issues.

People on the political left like to play word games. They are constantly redefining existing words (remember "tolerant"). They also rename certain activities. Liberal and progressive are more acceptable terms for a Socialist, Communist or Fascist. They sound less radical, more friendly, more helpful, less threatening.

Doesn't "social justice" sound better than "eliminating private property" or "transferring wealth"? When government **spending** falls out of favor, they call it government **investment**. When **General** Motors became **Government** Motors, they called it a **bailout**. In business terms it was a **government purchase, or acquisition**.

I do not mean to say that there are no politicians on the right that use language to manipulate the voter. The most difficult thing to find in Washington, D.C., is the truth. Professionals on both sides of the aisle like to **spin** the facts.

Here is an imaginary example of spin:

An army veteran of Desert Storm rides his Harley to visit a local zoo. While he is there he sees a small child fall into the lion's den. He leaps into the den himself. With only a stick he holds the lion at bay and hands the child up to his parents. When she is safe, he makes his exit. A reporter interviews him after the incident. The reporter does not like military people. He doesn't believe war is ever the right thing to do. The newspaper headline reads: "Army Vet Riding a Motorcycle Attacks an Immigrant at the Zoo and Steals His Lunch." It is true that the lion is an immigrant. Lions are not animals native to America. It is also true that he considered the child to be lunch.

This is "spin." The facts may be true, but they are reworded, rearranged or altered to mislead the audience.

My dad used to say: "You can tell you have become a star when you start believing your own publicity." Many Senators and Congressmen have been spinning the truth so long, they believe their own publicity.

There was a recent book written called *Liberal Fascism* by Jonah Goldberg. It compares the current attitudes and the roots of new liberals and new conservatives. Actually, today's liberals are, for the most part, economic Fascists or Socialists.

In Chapter 4, we bent the straight line political graph into a broken circle. Then we shifted it 90 degrees to the left, so it looks like this:

Figure 4

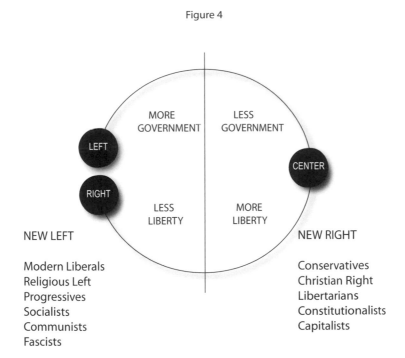

NEW LEFT

Modern Liberals
Religious Left
Progressives
Socialists
Communists
Fascists

NEW RIGHT

Conservatives
Christian Right
Libertarians
Constitutionalists
Capitalists

I always told people in middle management in our company not to be defensive if an employee asks, "Why are we doing this?" We should be able to tell them why.

If we can't give them a good reason, we need to ask ourselves, "Why are we doing this?"

A philosopher once noted, "The unexamined life is not worth living." Some people who would be really offended if they were called a fascist, a socialist or a communist actually approve of their ideas. Veterans who fought fascism in Europe, or communism and socialism in Korea and Vietnam, come home and vote for it here. Oh, it isn't listed on the ballot that way. Increased government ownership or control over our economy – and our daily life – is sold as a good thing.

Actors from Hollywood visit Cuba and Venezuela. They tell us how great communism and socialism work for the folks. If that is true, why don't we find Americans in overloaded, leaky boats trying to get to Cuba?

It is fair to say that the folks listed as the new left are working in the left side of our broken circle. Those shown as the new right are working in the right side of our broken circle. If you favor a **bigger government** and **less liberty**, you are on the left. If you favor a **smaller government** and **more liberty**, you are on the right.

Many people who are involved in politics don't know **why** they belong to a certain party. I went to a fish fry in a rural area of my district. It was a fundraiser for one of Southern Indiana's many volunteer fire departments. We had just finished walking a parade. After going through the food line, I picked up my drink and found a spot at a picnic table under a shelter house.

I was seated across from a young man, his wife and two children. We made some small talk about the parade and the weather. He told me he was president of a town council of a small community in the district. Then he said, "**I'm a Democrat**."

I responded, "**What does that mean**?"

Silence. Finally, I leaned over the table and said quietly, "**It's not a trick question**."

He changed the subject. A few minutes later he stopped in mid-sentence and said: "**My dad is a Democrat, we've always been Democrats**."

I understood that. I was a hereditary Democrat. My dad was a Democrat, his dad was a Democrat, and his dad's dad was a Democrat. Dad was what they used to call a "Reagan Democrat." He was a conservative Democrat.

I hope by the time you finish this book you will be able to tell someone why you are a _____ (fill in the blank). Are you a Democrat, a Republican, a Libertarian, a liberal, an independent conservative, a moderate, or other? Do you want more liberty? Or, are you willing to sell your liberty for an equal amount of security?

National healthcare (or **socialized medicine**) was rolled out the last time during the Clinton Administration. At the time, it hadn't yet occurred to me to run for Congress. A driver and I were talking one morning and he said: "That national healthcare sounds like a good idea. I'm sure some people could use that."

I responded: "There are two places I am confident you can find a lion today. One is in the African nation of

Kenya. If you look around on the Serengeti long enough you will find one.

"Or you can drive across the river to the Louisville Zoo. The zoo lion doesn't have to worry about **being** food or **finding** food. The zookeeper brings the zoo lion his food three or four times a day.

"The zoo lion has water and shelter, and if he gets sick, he has free healthcare. **The only thing he had to give up to get all those benefits was his liberty**.

"**We Americans are building our cage one bar at a time. And we won't really notice until the door slams shut**."

Ben Franklin, American patriot and revolutionary, said, "A man who will trade his liberty for a little temporary security deserves neither." Do you believe that? Are you willing to trade your liberty for security? The answer will help you fill in the blank.

8

So What About the Right Side of Our Circle?

The right side has common beliefs, and they have differences, just like the left. What they have in common is a belief in **smaller government** and **more individual liberty**.

The most fundamentalist of Christians, like the Amish, just want a government that will leave them alone. They live **in** this world, but do not want to be **of** this world. They do not look to FEMA after a disaster, and they are not looking for "free money." Very few Amish even vote.

In contrast to the Christian Right, the Religious Left is up to its neck in politics. In fact, I read one news report that the President was asking the Religious Left to help sell national health care. He had called on "progressive" (left side of circle) faiths to knock on doors and work at the grassroots level.

The Religious Left is constantly lobbying government to raise taxes and spend more of other people's money (to achieve so-called social justice). The Christian Right is more apt to start its own programs funded by voluntary contributions. They would be more likely to quote Matthew 22:21 where Christ said, "Give to Caesar what is Caesar's, and to God what is God's."

The Christian Right believes charity is voluntary. Some conservative denominations believe you obtain salvation (life after death) by grace (God's gift), and others by works (good deeds). But virtually no denomination on the right believes those "works" include lobbying for government money.

The Religious Left, on the other hand, believes government is a kind of non-denominational mega church, and taxes are the equivalent of tithing. But they don't believe the Biblical percentage is high enough.

The Libertarians, at the extreme, are virtually anarchists. (The anarchists would prefer no government at all.) Absolute individual freedom would be their ideal. The more mainstream Libertarians would like a return to the Constitutional Republic we were designed to be. Here again, the common belief is **less government** and **more liberty**.

The constitutionalists generally are compatible with the Christian Right on traditional marriage, abortion, euthanasia (assisted suicide) and most moral issues. They would agree with Libertarians on fiscal issues like balancing the budget. Here again, the common ground is **less government** and **more liberty**.

Capitalists are basically people who believe in the free exchange of goods and services between people. They believe it is **not** the business of government to engage in business. They range from the extreme of "laissez faire" (do as you please) to those who believe a reasonable level of regulation is necessary in a modern economy.

My Thorndike-Barnhart Dictionary says in part: laissez faire (lè say fèr) n. 1. The principle that trade, business, industry, etc., should operate with a minimum of regulation and interference by government (i.e., economy works best if private industry is not regulated and markets are free). 2. The principle of letting people do as they please. French: **Allowed to do as one pleases**.

The conservative is the most difficult to define. My Thorndike-Barnhart shows in part that a conservative is "a person who is opposed to change, either by nature or principle." As an adjective, the definition is "inclined to keep things as they are."

This does not describe most conservatives today. Most conservatives are in favor of change. The change they favor is completely different than the change that is taking place. They favor **less government** and **more liberty**.

Most conservatives believe government has grown too large and needs to be downsized. The people on the left side of the circle are **growing government and shrinking individual liberty**. The people on the right side want to **shrink government and restore liberty**.

What always surprises a wealthy liberal is a conservative who lives in a mobile home or a cabin up a "holler" in rural America. The pick-up truck parked out front probably has a gun rack in the back window. It likely has an American flag displayed prominently out front (except Texas, where it would be a Texas state flag).

The liberals believe that anyone who isn't living large should be an easy convert for the political left. The idea that there are Americans that still value their liberty, more than some government program or handout, just baffles them.

If they are unable to convince them that they can get something for nothing, they believe envy ought to do it. Surely there is some bait that will get them hooked and reeled into the waiting "left wing" political boat.

Frank Hines, president of Eagle International in the late-1970s and early-1980s, came from a "poor but proud" background. We used to buy our new motor coaches from Eagle International in Brownsville, Texas. In Chapter 10 we will deal with some of the tax issues that contributed to the plant closure. On one trip to Brownsville to pick up some new coaches, Frank invited us to his house for dinner.

I was sitting at his kitchen counter, not far from the front door, when the doorbell rang. Frank answered the door. Two kids were asking for donations. Frank replied that he didn't make donations.

He said his grass needed mowing, and he would pay them to mow it. He said his car needed washing, and he would pay them to wash it. But again, he said, he didn't make donations.

When he returned to the kitchen counter he said: "You probably heard the conversation at the front door, and you probably think I'm stingy. I want to tell you a story."

Frank went on: "I'm an Okie, born on a farm in Oklahoma. When I was in grade school three things happened in short order. The Depression set in, we had an extended drought, and my dad died.

"At Christmastime, we were in danger of losing the farm. A lady came driving up to our house. She was driving a nice car, wearing a fur coat, and carrying a box full of groceries.

"My mom met her at the door, told her she did not want the groceries, and she would appreciate it if this lady would load them up and leave. When she had driven away, my mom turned to me. She said; 'Frank, you probably think I was mean to that woman. I want to explain something to you.'

"She went on to tell me that the woman's husband owned a local lumber mill. She said: 'Your older brother has been trying to get a job in that lumber mill. Her husband says he can't afford to hire him. But they can afford to buy those groceries and bring them out here.'

"She went on: 'Frank, nothing comes for free in life. Everything has a price. You will pay for those groceries with your pride.'"

Frank told me: "When you are young, poor and hungry, a life lesson like that sticks with you. Even today, I can't give somebody anything but an opportunity to earn what they need."

Frank said people would ask him when he was a kid, "What do you want to be when you grow up?" He would tell them, a doctor. They would say, "You big dumb Okie, you can't be a doctor. So, I became an engineer." He said, "If I hadn't listened to those dummies I would have been a doctor."

During my congressional campaign someone wrote a letter to the editor (LTE) to our local newspaper. The letter said I didn't care about poor people. Our most senior coach operator, Beany Smith, sent in a response. He said that he qualified as "poor people." When I hired him, he was sleeping in the back of a 1966 Dodge Dart station wagon.

He went on to say that since I hired him, he got married, bought a home, raised two sons, owned two cars, a bass boat and a pontoon boat. He said the best thing you can do for poor people is to make them middle class.

The local paper would not publish his response. They said it was too close to the election. It wasn't too close for an attack, but it was too close for a response. Since the majority of the news media (newspaper, television, radio, etc.) is left of center, it follows that the majority of information will be slanted that way. Media bias is a completely different subject; Bernie Goldberg wrote a great book about it titled Bias.

Ideas from the left side of our circle get more free ink in the newspaper and free air time on television than those coming from the right. Even many people with advanced degrees don't get it. A left-wing PhD called a young man a Fascist one day because the young man said he believed citizens had a constitutional right to keep and bear arms.

My dad used to ask, "Is he stupid, or does he think I am?" Individual liberty is as far from fascism as you can get. Adolph Hitler confiscated privately owned firearms in the middle 1930s. Fascists believe in total government control. It is difficult to control people who are armed.

It is individual liberty that conservatives want to restore. It is American culture and a common language that conservatives want to preserve. Economic liberty is important to conservatives as well.

This country has become so focused on diversity that it has lost sight of competence. We have become so focused on multi-culturalism, we forgot about American culture. *E pluribus unum* was supposed to mean "From many, one." We were a melting pot. Immigrants who used to come here, for the most part, wanted to be Americans.

Many immigrants who come here today don't want to **be** Americans, they just want to **live** in America. Others want us to adapt to their customs, their beliefs, and their language.Some have even filed lawsuits to require us to conform to their religious beliefs. They demand more consideration than an American would get in their home country.

Most conservatives want to preserve the United States Constitution. They want to restore and preserve individual liberty, particularly economic liberty. Most want to have opportunity for all Americans.

Conservatives are not opposed to change. They are opposed to bad change. They oppose change for the sake of change. Conservatives are opposed to socialism, communism, fascism and collectivism. Most of them believe America is fast becoming a hybrid socialist/fascist economy. The leftists are buying the companies they can with government funds (provided by the taxpayer), and controlling those they can not buy.

Most conservatives are not opposed to foreign intervention when American interests or American security is at stake. I am persuaded that it is time to leave both Afghanistan and Iraq. We should leave a force sufficient to protect our diplomats and other Americans that will remain.

We cannot fight an unconventional enemy with conventional forces. We need sufficient human intelligence and surveillance to make sure terrorist training camps are not returning to Afghanistan. If they do, we need to take them out. That does not require a large footprint of conventional forces.

We cannot be the world's police force. Our economy is not healthy. We cannot afford either the loss of life or the financial drain of prosecuting the war on terror with large, conventional military forces.

To me, conservatism is about common sense. There is a prayer that goes like this: *God grant me the courage to change the things I can, the serenity to accept the things I cannot change, and the wisdom to know the difference.* Modern liberals lack wisdom. They seem to believe the reason that repressive forms of government fail is they didn't have the right people in charge.

Lord Acton, the British admiral and philosopher, said: "Power has a tendency to corrupt; absolute power corrupts absolutely." Or, as Thomas Jefferson put it: "Where the people fear the government there is tyranny, where the government fears the people there is liberty."

Virtually all of us have been treated badly by some government bureaucrat that had no fear of a citizen. We are rarely treated like customers – because we aren't. A customer can go elsewhere.

So, what are you thinking? Are you more of a left-side or right-side kind of person?

9
Where Does Capitalism Fit Into Our Broken Circle?

The year 1776 was important for more than one reason. The same year Thomas Jefferson penned our Declaration of Independence, a guy named Adam Smith wrote *Wealth of Nations*.

Smith was a professor of Moral Philosophy at Edinburgh University in Scotland. His first book called *Theory of Moral Sentiments* was published in 1759. It was about human nature. Our guy Smith wasn't an accountant, or an economist. (They hadn't invented economics yet.) Some people call him the Father of Capitalism, or the Founder of Modern Economics.

Most good book titles tell you what a book is about. Smith was curious to know why some nations were wealthier than others. He wanted to know why prices went up and down.

To make a long story short, he developed the theory of **supply and demand**. He actually called it supply and **effective** demand. This was what he called the **invisible hand** that controlled prices.

If there is a lot of stuff for sale, more than people actually want or need, the price goes down. If the demand for something goes up, and the supply doesn't, prices go up.

The idea of the invisible hand was that the reason prices went up and down couldn't be seen. But it didn't happen by accident either. Increases or reductions in either the **supply** of something or the **demand** for something causes price changes.

The best example of this was related to me by a friend in California. A few years back there was an oil refinery fire in California. It quickly reduced the amount of gasoline that was for sale in the area.

My friend bought his gas at a small independent convenience store. He drove in one morning after the refinery fire to find the price for gasoline was up almost 50 cents a gallon.

He asked the owner of the store if he wasn't afraid people would stop doing business with him. His answer is a good example of the invisible hand of supply and demand.

He replied: "Until the refinery is repaired I am on an allocation. In other words, my gasoline supplier is limiting the number of gallons of gas I will get to sell each week.

"If I run out of gas, no one will stop here. If no one stops here for gas, I won't sell any bread, milk, coffee, candy bars or anything else. **I can't run out of gasoline**."

He went on: "I know how many gallons I'm going to get. I read my pumps every hour. If my customers are buying so much that I am going to run out, I raise the price a nickel a gallon.

"I keep raising the price a nickel a gallon every hour until I am pumping the amount I will have available to sell. If I'm pumping too slow, I drop the price a nickel a gallon to make sure I sell all the gas I have available.

"If my price gets too high, **some people** may go somewhere else looking for cheaper gas. But, if I run out of gasoline **nobody will stop**. If I am out of gas, I'm out of business. **I can't run out of gasoline**."

My personal definition of capitalism is "The free exchange of goods and services between people." In the example above, no one was forced to buy his gas. If they thought there was a better deal down the street, they were free to go there.

On the other hand, the store owner wasn't forced to sell at the price the buyer wanted to pay. Raising or lowering the price per gallon was the owner's method for balancing supply and demand.

So how do nations get wealthier? Smith said, "Anyone who **produces** more than he **consumes** makes a nation wealthier." Put another way, people who create a surplus make a nation wealthier. He also said, "All civilizations are built on a surplus of food."

In 1900, 95 out of 100 Americans lived on the land. They lived in rural areas and farmed. In other words, **it took 95 of us to feed 100 of us**. That 5-percent surplus of food allowed some of us to go do something else.

One hundred years later, the situation had reversed itself. By 2000, it took less than five of us to feed 100 of us. Farm machinery like tractors, combines, corn planters and pickers, plus improved farming techniques, allowed more than 95 of us to go do something else.

By producing more than he consumes, the American farmer has made our nation wealthier. Any person who produces more than they consume makes a nation wealthier. This also means that people who **consume** more than they produce **make a nation poorer**.

Bureaucrats, for the most part, produce nothing. Any time we are adding government jobs, our communities, our states and our nation are all getting poorer. We cannot become a nation of consumers. We have to continue to produce things.

An assembly-line worker at the Allison Transmission Plant in Indianapolis creates more wealth for America than virtually any member of Congress. If we are going to get America back on the right economic course, we have to create productive jobs, not overhead jobs.

Unfortunately, **our economy is becoming a fascist economy**. Government regulations over hours worked, rates paid, promotions, hiring and firing, product specifications and so on give private employers less control over their businesses every year.

With the acquisition of **Government Motors** (GM), the new left has shown themselves to be a hybrid of the classic left and classic right. If government can **own** it they will; if they can't **own** it, they will **control** it.

Capitalism is a state of **economic liberty**. It is dying a slow death at the hands of the new left and their hired help.

10

In Our Republic, Government's Job is to Referee the Game, not to Determine Who Wins or Loses

Only an extreme radical would suggest that we could live in a society with no rules. These people are called anarchists. Can you imagine playing any sport with no rules?

The Rule of Law applies even in sporting events. The game is played in accordance with a pre-determined set of rules. The rules are established **with the consent of the governed**.

A baseball umpire cannot decide to give a batter four strikes instead of three before declaring he has struck out.

A basketball referee cannot decide to take points scored by one team and give them to the other team.

The spectators cannot decide by majority vote to give their favorite team the win.

The majority in the stands cannot decide. "It wouldn't be fair" for a 0-8 team to lose another game. They cannot grant that team a win based on a sympathy vote.

The ruler cannot give a thumbs-up or a thumbs-down to the gladiator as he did in ancient Rome. America's Founders did not want to be ruled by one person or a group of people ... that is why they chose the rule of law.

Thomas Jefferson authored the Declaration of Independence. He contributed to the Constitutional Convention and served as our third President. In his Presidential Inaugural Address given in 1801, President Thomas Jefferson said, "A wise and frugal government ... **one that shall prevent men from injuring one another**" is the best form of government.

Wisdom is best described as the understanding of human nature. Being frugal means not spending money or resources unnecessarily or wastefully. Our current government officials rarely show wisdom, and very few people would say that government makes the best use of our tax dollars.

Junior Achievement is an organization that educates young people about our economic system. At one time they had a program called "Project Business." Business people would go into an eighth-grade classroom to teach with the economics teacher. I volunteered to teach such a class.

During the fall semester, I asked the students if they had a football team. "Sure," they said.

"Did they play last Friday night?"

"Sure did."

"Did they win or lose?"

"They lost."

"How do you know?"

"How do we know what?"

"How do you know whether they won or lost?

"Oh, the other team scored more points."

"So the scoreboard told you that your team lost?"

"Yes."

"How long do you think people would play football if we took the scoreboard down?"

"Not very long," they agreed.

"How many people do you think would come to watch?"

"What would be the point?" They thought the game would be pointless with no goal.

"If I put two teams on the field, and I guaranteed neither of them would lose, which one would win?"

"Neither of them."

"Your team lost last week. Does that mean they will lose next week?"

"No."

We have people in our government today who want to control the score, not referee the game. They want to choose who wins the game and they want to choose who plays. Some of them don't care about the game at all. They don't care if anybody plays, or if anybody watches, or if anybody wins.

If these folks were allowed to make all the rules, they would make the goal posts three stories high and eighteen inches wide. They would make the basketball hoop smaller than a basketball.

I listened to a speech given by a retired National Football League (NFL) referee. He said a lot of people say, "The trouble with football is that it is not enough like real life.

"I say the problem with real life is that it isn't enough like football. If everyone got up every day and gave the same level of commitment, determination and effort as a football team, what kind of country would we have?"

Part of the process of developing a winning team is finding the right players. Part of the process is training the players you have. Part of winning is keeping the best players when you get them. An unfortunate part of developing a championship team is removing the players that do not fit.

Hiring and firing are a necessary part of business life. I have never liked doing either. When I hired someone, I knew, despite my best efforts, some people were not going to work out. Sometimes the employee understood it was not a good fit and they quit. This meant we had to hire again. Sometimes they would not quit, and we had to ask them to leave. Sometimes we had to insist they leave.

When you fire an employee you get different reactions: sometimes silence, sometimes anger, sometimes it's hurt. A young man I had to let go after some incidents and accidents was so upset, he was crying. I told him I wasn't telling him he was a bad person. I was telling him he wasn't a professional driver.

I told him my daughter was first chair, first violin, the concert mistress of a youth orchestra. I can't play a note on a violin. That does not mean she is a good person and I am a bad person. It means she is a violinist and I am not.

I told him, "I'm not telling you that you are a bad person. I'm saying you are not a professional driver, and you will never be good at it. There is a big world out there, and a lot of things you can do for a living. There is something you will be very good at, and you need to find it. Professional driving is not your calling."

Part of our problem today is that the government is too involved in our economy. They want to control the whole process, virtually start to finish. They are involved in hiring, firing, promotions, demotions, time off, hours worked, benefits provided, wages paid – virtually every economic decision.

If we continue at this pace, we will have a referee for every player. The winner will be chosen by committee, or we will just take the scoreboard down. No one will want to play or watch, and America's team will be defeated in a world marketplace.

Congress passes too much "enabling" legislation. They let the referees make the rules. They constantly change the rule book in an attempt to control the outcome of the game. They want to control who plays and who does not. And "we the people" tolerate, and sometimes encourage, this **economic fascism**. We would not put up with it in professional sports.

What if we had a rule in football that said each team had to have so many skinny players? Or a basketball team had to have so many short players? How could a football team play with 22 referees on the field?

The government referees need to understand, fans do not come to watch them. Fans come to watch the game. Kids do not collect baseball umpire cards. As stated earlier, my dad always said, "You can tell you have become a star when you start believing your own publicity."

Government-elected and hired officials are a necessary part of our society. However, they do not create wealth. They do not create jobs, and they do not score any points. They believe too much of their own publicity.

Again quoting Adam Smith: "Anyone who produces more than he consumes makes a nation wealthier." A bulldozer operator makes a nation wealthier than a member of Congress.

We need a government that establishes reasonable rules in accordance with the supreme "Rule of Law," the United States Constitution. Then, they need to get out of the way and let citizens play the game.

It's important to have rules, but it's equally important to preserve the game.

The level of individual liberty that was possible when our Constitution was written in the 18th century is not possible today. Even if we use President Thomas Jefferson's standard from his inaugural address in 1801, there are more ways today for men "to injure one another."

We have nuclear waste, toxic chemicals, and more people living in the same space. More government control is a necessary part of a modern technological society. But unnecessary government control makes American products cost more, and it often lowers quality. This means fewer American jobs.

Congress and the bureaucrats keep changing the rules. We wouldn't tolerate it in sports, why do we put up with it in government?

"The majority in the stands cannot decide
'It wouldn't be fair for a 0-8 team to lose
another game.'
They cannot grant that team a win
based on a sympathy vote."

11
The Taxman

If you drive a car, I'll tax the street
If you try to sit, I'll tax your seat
If you get too cold, I'll tax the heat
If you take a walk, I'll tax your feet
Taxman!
Cos I'm the taxman, yeah I'm the taxman
(The Beatles)

Go get your last pay stub. Go ahead, I'll wait. Now, I have a question for you. Would you rather be paid the **gross** amount shown, or the **net**? If your income were to go from the net to the gross, that would be a nice raise wouldn't it?

I still remember my first real paycheck. I bagged groceries for Publix Supermarket for $1 an hour, 24 hours a week. My **$24 gross** income was **$18.54 net**. This was quite a shock, since I expected to be paid $24.

My point is this: The FairTax eliminates all payroll withholding taxes. No more Social Security Tax, Medicaid or Medicare Tax. No Federal Income Tax would be withheld from your pay. If you make $1,000, you get $1,000.

So now your question is: If I'm not paying any taxes, how do we run the government? What about the Social Security trust fund? What about the military?

The Social Security trust fund is a joke. Actually, it isn't a joke. It is too serious to be a joke. It is merely an accounting gimmick. Any money not needed to pay current benefits is borrowed by some other governmental department.

Here is how this works: Let's say you have your employer deduct your 401k contribution from your pay every week. But, at the end of every month, your employer takes the money out and leaves an IOU. Your employer would be jailed if caught.

When you get ready to retire, all you will have is a bunch of IOUs. So, in order for you to retire, your children and grandchildren have to support you. Some bureaucrat took the money and left the IOUs. The next generation will have to support their children, and their parents (you).

This is the way your Social Security trust fund works. It is kinda like a generational musical-chair game. Some day the music will stop, and that generation won't have a chair (no money). It is a government-sponsored Ponzi scheme. It works like the one Bernie Madoff was running except it is legal. I didn't say **moral**, I said **legal**.

Anyway, we were talking about taxes. The Fair-Tax eliminates all Federal Tax withholding, **and it eliminates the Internal Revenue Service** (affectionately known as the IRS). Think about that. **No more 1040 forms**. **No more W-2s**; for you small-business types, **no more 941 forms**, **no quarterly estimates**. April 15 would be a good day to go fishing.

Some say it can't be done. Check your history books and the U.S. Constitution. This country ran with no federal income tax from 1789 when our Constitution was adopted, until the Sixteenth Amendment was ratified in 1913. Think about that. **One hundred and twenty-four years** with no Federal Income Tax or payroll withholding.

OK. So you do not believe in the tooth fairy. **Where is the government going to get its money**? You, dear sheep, will pay a National Sales Tax of 23 percent.

One night I talked about the FairTax on the "Huckabee Show" on Fox News. I said: "We should not call this the FairTax. We should call it **the American Job Creation and Retention Act**."

Right now, **Chinese products reach the cash register** (point of retail sale) **with Chinese taxes** (or no taxes, or subsidies) imbedded (included) in their price.

American products reach the cash register with an average of 22 percent American taxes imbedded in their price. This gives the Chinese-made products a price advantage over American products.

The FairTax levels the tax playing field. Both the Chinese product and the American product will be taxed at the same 23 percent. **But, the American product will be 22 percent (on average) cheaper to produce**. Why? Because companies involved in domestic production will have lower costs.

Remember what Adam Smith said: "Anyone who produces more than he consumes makes a nation wealthier." We can't become a nation of consumers. We have to continue making things. A nation that cannot manufacture the things it needs to defend itself will become defenseless.

I am not going to dwell on the FairTax. There is The Fair Tax book by Neil Boortz and Congressman John Linder if you want to learn more. And a second book responds to critics and naysayers.

Folks, we can eliminate billions of dollars that are spent every year for operating expenses, forms and processing at the I.R.S. We can make American products more competitive here and abroad.

Our economy doesn't need a government bailout … it doesn't need a short-term stimulus. Our economy needs a stable, long-term, tax and regulatory structure that encourages growth and productivity.

Short-term stimulus sounds like something a drug addict is looking for. We need long-term opportunity, to produce long-lasting prosperity.

The equipment and tools necessary to provide jobs for American citizens require long-term investments. Buildings and machinery can be a 30-year investment and more. Railroad engines, tow boats, barges and similar transportation equipment can be more than 20 years. Buses, trucks, trailers are 10-to 20-year investments.

Americans cannot make 10-, 20- or 30-**year** investments on 10-, 20- or 30-**month** tax policy.

If all this is true, why won't Congress enact the FairTax? Answer: **Loss of control**. Lobbyists hate it. Fifty percent of the lobbying in Washington, D.C., is directed at the Tax Code.

This means that the number of lobbyists would drop by 50 percent, or they would make 50 percent less money. The prospect of either doesn't appeal to lobbyists. So, they give their clients at least a hundred reasons they should oppose it.

Members of Congress would become less important as well. At least 50 percent of what they do is changing the Tax Code. The chairman of the Ways and Means Committee wouldn't have much to do. They have to keep on herding and shearing – so they want to keep the system as it is.

"Folks we can eliminate billions of dollars that are spent every year for operating expenses, forms and processing at the IRS. We can make American products more competitive here and abroad."

12

A Subsidized Chicken in the Pot Today Means a lot of Feathers Tomorrow

Unfortunately, Congressional decisions are made every day by people who have **zero** practical experience creating private-sector jobs or balancing budgets. Some of these decisions are made by elected members, and some by unelected committee lawyers and staff people.

In this economic downturn, Liberals in Congress talk about "short-term stimulus" to "jump start" our economy. They talk about it like it is a car with a dead battery. If they just "jump start" it, we can drive happily off into the economic sunset.

The current batch of people running our country reminds me of 1960s radicals. One of the slogans of those radicals was "no quoting." Everyone had to be "authentic." In other words, everybody who went before them got it wrong, and they were going to invent an entirely new and different society.

The problem with this thinking is two-fold. First, you lose the opportunity to build on what past generations did right. And second, you lose the advantage of avoiding their mistakes.

Benjamin Franklin certainly wasn't afraid of trying something new. He was the oldest participant at our Constitutional Convention where a new form of government was drawn up. Ben Franklin invented swim fins, bifocal glasses, the Franklin stove, and experimented with electricity.

One of his famous sayings was: "Experience teaches a dear school, but a fool will learn in no other." He wasn't afraid to try something new. But, he took advantage of the experience of others to save himself time and trouble.

With this in mind, let's take a look at how the economic stimulus plan of the early 1980s worked. The Investment Tax Credit and Energy Tax Credit programs in the early 1980s were designed to "stimulate" the manufacturing part of our economy. In that respect it was like cash-for-clunkers.

Instead of a cash payment, the 1980s program was made up of temporary tax credits. If your company didn't need the tax credits, they could be sold for cash. Individuals and corporations that were making money and owed taxes could buy tax credits from not-for-profits, government-owned businesses, or companies that were losing money.

At the time, I compared it to allowing people who were on public assistance to sell their dependent allowance to someone who was earning their money, and owed taxes.

Can you imagine walking through a government housing project knocking on doors? It would go like this:

"Good morning, ma'am, I'm John Taxpayer. I would like to lower my taxes. If you aren't paying taxes, can I buy your dependent child deduction? Since it will save me in taxes, I'll pay you $1,500 in cash for each child you let me claim."

So, how well did the temporary tax credits work? For example: Like cash-for-clunkers, it lowered the cost of buying a new vehicle for bus companies. But, instead of providing an incentive to get rid of the old one, the system encouraged companies to keep them.

At the time a new intercity motor coach (like a Greyhound bus) was selling for about $150,000. The tax credits lowered the selling price to $120,000 immediately. And it encouraged companies to keep the old bus.

The Investment Tax Credit (ITC) was allowed for buying a new intercity bus. The additional Energy Tax Credit (ETC) was allowed only if the company kept the old one.

We were buying our motor coaches at the time from Eagle International in Brownsville, Texas. The tax credits certainly "stimulated" their business. They were building new buses at the rate of about one per day. You had to wait 18 months for a new one.

When the tax credits expired, their production dropped from 360-370 per year to 50-54 per year. They attempted to build buses for transit (city buses) and then went out of business altogether.

When the tax credits expired, the cost of a new intercity motor coach immediately increased by 20 percent (more than $30,000 each). And the market was flooded with used buses that the bus companies had been encouraged to keep.

There is a company in Jeffersonville, Indiana, called Jeffboat. They build barges, towboats and other similar marine equipment. The temporary tax credits "stimulated" their business as well. They were launching a new barge a day into the Ohio River.

When the tax credits expired, they closed the plant for three years! They went from 360-370 units a year to **zero** for three years. At least they finally reopened, Eagle is gone permanently. These are two companies I can speak about. One we did business with, and one in our community. I'm sure there are many similar stories.

When you produce more donuts than the market can use, it is a one-day problem. Pitch the excess (or give them to a homeless shelter) and the market surplus disappears.

When government "stimulus" causes too many long-term assets to be produced, it can take years to work through the system. Barges, buses, cars, trucks will be around for years.

Short-term manipulation of the marketplace can (and does) produce long-term problems.

Cash-for-clunkers "stimulated" the sale of certain new cars. And it drove up the price of used cars. But it did not address the long-term issues of taxes, regulation and red tape that strangle American manufacturing and kill American jobs.

The one thing people must have to invest in the future is stability. They need predictable, stable tax rates and regulatory policy. No one wants to invest in the future unless they believe it will be better than today. If they don't see anything good in their future, they won't invest in it.

Right now, people who would normally be investing in machinery and buildings, and providing new jobs, see nothing but feathers down the road. The American Left has created that environment, and they will now use it as an excuse to take over as much of our economy as possible.

They have transferred General Motors and Chrysler from the private sector to government. They have acquired or control large chunks of our banking and insurance sectors. Now they have set their sights on the medical sector – then communication and transportation.

All this is socialism, "never called by its right name," as the Fabian Socialist George Bernard Shaw would say.

What the American economy needs is long-term stability. Predictable, simple and stable taxes; common sense and stable regulations; predictable, reasonable, energy costs, are all necessary ingredients to be a strong and growing economy.

We need to maximize tax payers and minimize tax users. This administration, and this Congress, are punishing taxpayers and increasing tax users. This is a formula for turning America into a third-world country.

"We need to maximize taxpayers and minimize tax users. This Administration and this Congress is punishing **tax payers** and increasing **tax users**. This is a formula for turning America in to a third world country."

13

Freedom's Just Another Word
for Nothing Left to Lose

Freedom's just another word for nothing left to lose
("Me and Bobby McGee"—Janice Joplin)

I prefer to use the word **liberty** rather than **freedom**. As Janice Joplin pointed out, only people who have nothing to lose can be completely free. If you have no property, you have no responsibility to maintain it. You can sleep under a bridge and have no responsibility to report for work. If you don't have a family, you have no family responsibilities.

The dictionary definitions of "liberty" and "freedom" are very long, and they are very similar. There is a sentence under **"freedom"** that helps to define the difference: **"Too great liberty**; lack of restraint; frankness. *We did not like the freedom of his manner.*" There is one under **"liberty"** that sheds some light as well: "Permission granted to a sailor to go ashore, usually for not more than 48 hours. *His liberty stopped for getting drunk.*"

Freedom does **whatever it wants to do**. Liberty does **what it should do**. Liberty and responsibility go hand-in-hand. They are like heads and tails of the same coin. I believe freedom is **undisciplined**; liberty is **self-disciplined**; government is **imposed discipline**. Our Founders understood the difference.

John Adams signed our Declaration of Independence. He was our nation's first Vice President under President George Washington. He was our second President and author of the Massachusetts State Constitution. Adams was one of the first 56 Americans to risk everything for liberty. He understood the nature of liberty.

In 1789, John Adams said, "Our Constitution was designed for a **moral and religious people** … it is wholly inadequate to govern any other." Or, as James Madison, our fourth President and author of the U.S. Constitution, observed, **"If men were angels, we would have no need of government**."

There are two ways to think about the term "self-government." One is: "We the People" govern ourselves **collectively** in accordance with the United States Constitution. The other is: "We the People" govern ourselves **individually** in accordance with the Judeo/Christian tradition. Adams and Madison were referring to the concept of individual **government of the self**.

One of the companies I founded is called The Free Enterprise System. Free Enterprise now operates motor coaches in chartered service throughout the United States and Canada. It also operates contract shuttle operations.

In June 1976, Free Enterprise took over the operations of Home Transit and Daisy Line. Home Transit transported commuters and shoppers around New Albany, Clarksville and Jeffersonville, Indiana. Daisy Line took people from those Southern Indiana communities to Louisville, Kentucky, and back.

I named the company The Free Ente
tem **because we refused to accept any
assistance from local, state or federal go**
From 1976 to 1983 we operated this transit
without any government assistance. In 198?
sit Authority of River City (TARC) took over
operations. TARC is a government-owned bus

The other reason I named the com
Enterprise is that I believe in the marketplac
sonal definition of capitalism is: **the free ex
goods and services between people**. In oui
system, people should be able to freely buy
legal product or service. The price should be d
by the buyer and the seller, not a bureaucrat

Free Enterprise contracts to take group?
wherever they might want to go in the United ?
Canada. Passengers may be a group of senio
a corporate group, a church group, or it may k
of school children going on an educational trij

When we take school children on a
must have adult supervision, or chaperones,
with them. The number of chaperones requir
with the age of the students. Small elementa:
children need an adult to each three or four ?
By the time they reach high school, a chapero:
or so young people is normally adequate.

As children grow closer to adulthood, tl
less supervision. Their individual **self-di**
gradually replaces the **imposed discipline**
stant supervision. In effect, **children earn tl
erty by demonstrating their responsibility**. T

imposed discipline shrinks as their self-discipline
ows.

When people become adults, John Adam's idea of
dividual **government of the self** is supposed to take
er. Adults are supposed to have their bags packed.
ey are expected to show up on time. They are expected
be able to follow directions without supervision. Adult
oups do not have chaperones.

**Modern liberals want citizens to live in a con-
ant state of childhood**. They want government to be
e parents. It is their goal to have a nation of depen-
nt citizens with bureaucrats acting as chaperones.
e more dependent we are, the more chaperones we
ed. The more chaperones we have, the less liberty we
joy. It is a downward spiral.

My paternal great-grandfather Martin was the first
odrel to arrive in America. He died in Perry County, Indi-
a, in July 1919. His obituary noted that "... although
e was born in a foreign land, **he was intensely Ameri-
an. He was ready to assist the government in any-
hing it would undertake**." Isn't that an interesting
oncept – weak government, strong people?

As late as 1960, President John F. Kennedy said,
**Ask not what your country can do for you, ask what
ou can do for your country**." Today, political cam-
aigns often become an auction, with each candidate
aising his bid on what your country will do for you.
ow many new laws they will pass, how many new pro-
rams they will start, how much more "help" they will
ive, becomes the campaign focus.

The modern liberal will tell the voter, "You can't trust business types; they seek profit." What they do not tell you is that modern **liberals seek control**. They seek **control** over your earnings, **control** over your property, and **control** over your daily life. They sell their quest for control as "helping people." Remember, they love sheep.

For every responsibility you hand over to government, you lose an equal measure of liberty. Every time you become more dependent, the number of government chaperones increases.

The modern Socialist does not take power with bullets, he does it with ballots. They set the trap with appealing bait and wait for the citizen to spring it. If liberty is to survive, it must be defended with words, with actions, and with ballots.

Individual self-government is necessary to maintain individual liberty. The Founders signed the Declaration of Independence, not the Declaration of ***Dependence***.

"We the People" do not need more laws. You cannot compensate for moral decay by passing more laws. We do not need to transfer more control over our daily lives to our government. **We need a spiritual revival, a moral re-awakening, and a rediscovery of civic and personal responsibility**.

When we buried my dad, I gave his eulogy. In part, I said, "**If everyone lived as he lived, we wouldn't need a police department, jails or armies**." This is the America John Adams was referring to.

Modern liberals and atheists want God taken out of the classroom, the courtroom, the boardroom and any place you find Him in the public square. He is the cornerstone of the Republic. Moral and religious training prevents theft; government punishes theft. "Thou shalt not steal" is a spiritual commandment. "Grand theft auto" is a civil crime.

Liberty must take personal responsibility, or die a slow death at the hands of elected officials and bureaucrats. You have to ask yourself, how many bureaucratic chaperones do you want traveling through life with you?

If you value liberty as the Founders did, you need to choose people who value liberty to serve as elected officials.

14

If We Aren't a Christian Nation, Why is Moses (the Lawgiver) Looking at the Speaker of the U.S. House?

I was listening to talk radio one morning when a caller announced flatly, "Our founders intended to establish a secular government." Our current president has said, "We are not a Christian nation." We are a Christian nation. We **are** a Christian nation that tolerates people of other faiths or no faith at all. However, the new left is working hard to change that.

There is a difference between avoiding a state-sponsored religion, and establishing a Godless government. The Founders were trying to balance God and country.

In the First Amendment to the United States Constitution, they prohibited the United States Congress from imposing a specific religion. **"Congress shall make no law respecting an establishment of religion."** They did not want Congress to pass a law that said we are all going to be Baptists, or Catholics, or Methodists.

The First Amendment also says, "... **or, prohibiting the free exercise thereof** ..." So the amendment strikes a balance. In law today, lawyers talk about the "establishment" clause. When was the last time you heard discussion about the "prohibition" clause?

We had a federal judge issue an order prohibiting anyone from saying "Jesus Christ" on the floor of the Indiana State House of Representatives. Not Buddha, or

Allah – just Jesus Christ. What is that, if it is not pro-hibiting the free exercise thereof?

If our Founders were atheists (people who deny the existence of God), why would they write and sign a document (our Declaration of Independence) that speaks of "**nature's God**" and states that people are "endowed by their **Creator** with certain unalienable rights"?

Would they do so "with a firm reliance on the protection of **Divine Providence**"? Would they even acknowledge such a thing as divine providence?

Many people seem to think that hanging the Ten Commandments in a public place is a problem. Hanging them up is not a problem. **Enforcing them would be a real problem**.

For example: If we were to enforce the Seventh Commandment (Thou shalt not commit adultery) in today's society, overcrowding in the jails would have an entirely new meaning.

If we were to enforce the Ninth Commandment (Thou shalt not lie), there might not be enough Sena-tors or Congressman left to conduct business. Corpo-rate America would not fare very well either.

If we were to enforce the Tenth Commandment (Thou shalt not covet) – there would not be enough socialists left on the street to make the next election cycle competitive.

I believe the greatest hazard to the separation of church and state is not Judeo-Christian icons displayed in public places. It isn't "**In God We Trust**" on our currency, or **"under God"** in the Pledge of Allegiance to our flag. The greatest hazard is mixing Caesar's money with God's money. **Using the power of the government to require charitable giving is a really bad idea**.

As more government money is provided for "faith-based" organizations, they become more secular in nature. As they become more dependent on government to sustain themselves, **their faith in man grows and their faith in God shrinks**.

I know, you want to know what I meant in the chapter heading – "Why is Moses (the Lawgiver) Looking at the Speaker of the U.S. House?"

The Speaker of the House chooses speakers pro tem (temporary speakers) to oversee the business of the house in his or her absence. The speaker pro tem is, in effect, Speaker of the House for short periods of time.

As you might imagine, the House chamber looks different from the speaker's rostrum than it does from the floor. The first time I was temporary speaker, I took the opportunity to look around the chamber.

After recognizing another member of Congress to speak, I looked up at the visitor's gallery. The gallery is a balcony which is difficult to see from the floor. Over each entrance door to the gallery there is a bas relief (raised likeness) of some person in history. Each likeness is from the neck up, facing left or right, with their name below.

To the left rear of the Speaker is Thomas Jefferson. To the right rear of the Speaker is George Mason.

Jefferson is a left profile, Mason is a right profile. Everyone is left or right – **all but one**.

Over the center entrance door to the visitor's gallery, full-faced, looking directly down at the Speaker is **Moses**. Why would secular people put **Moses** in this position? Why would secular people make his likeness full-faced, looking directly at the speaker?

The first time I walked into the Science Committee hearing room, I noticed gold leaf lettering on the wood-paneled wall behind the members, facing the audience. "Where there is no vision, the people perish" (Proverbs 29:18) was written on the wall. Why would a secular people put Bible scripture on the wall of a committee room?

"In God We Trust" is on a bronze plaque in the lobby of the Longworth House Office Building. The rotunda of the capitol has a mural of Pocahontas being baptized.

If you could scale the **outside** of the Washington Monument, if you could climb all 555 feet of white marble, you would find a small aluminum pyramid on top. On the east face of that aluminum pyramid – in a place that only God can see it when the sun rises – are the Latin words *Laus Deo*, **"praise be to God"** in English.

One might argue that **"In God We Trust"** does not refer necessarily to a Judeo/Christian God. One cannot, however, argue that Moses was not a Jew. Neither can an argument be made that Proverbs 29:18 is not found in the Christian Bible.

God is the cornerstone of the American republic. Our individual rights were God-granted. Our second President John Adams said, "Our Constitution was designed for a moral and religious people. It is wholly inadequate to govern any other."

A moral and religious people do not require many laws. Moses only brought 10 down from the mountain. An immoral people cannot pass enough laws to govern themselves. **Liberty requires government of the self**. James Madison, author of the United States Constitution and our fourth President, said, **"If men were angels, we would have no need of government**."

These people who are attacking Christianity on a daily basis are undermining our republic. If we are not a Christian nation, why is Moses (the lawgiver) looking at the Speaker of the House?

"God is the cornerstone of the American Republic. **Our individual rights were God granted**."

15

Faith Should Give You a Reason to Live and a Reason to Die, not a Reason to Murder

In 1952, Wittaker Chambers wrote a book called *Witness*. Chambers was a committed Communist for longer than a decade. Something he wrote in that book changed the way I look at communism. By seeing communism in a different light, the world looks different.

Chambers wrote that some people mistake communism for an **economic system**. Other people mistake communism for a **political system**. He went on to say, "**It is neither of these**." Communism, he said, is a **faith**. His definition of faith was it was something that "**Gives a man a reason to live and a reason to die**."

He went on to say that there were two major faiths in the world at that time (1952): Communism and Christianity ... **faith in man** or **faith in God**. I picked up a copy of the Communist Manifesto. It states that "Communism abolishes eternal truths, **it abolishes all religion**, and all morality." In classic communism, the state replaces the church.

In classic communism, the **state is the church**.

By great faiths, or **major faiths**, I think he meant faiths that had the **will** and the **means** to project their worldviews worldwide. In the middle of the 20th century, Christian missionaries were spreading the Gospel all over the globe. Communists were practicing conversion by the sword all over the world as well.

What has changed in little more than a half century is the discovery of large deposits of oil in the Middle East. This enormous influx of wealth from the sale of oil created a third major faith: **Islam**. Islam always had the **will** to project itself; it had done so before. But it had lost the **means**. Oil revenue restored the means.

In a traditional Islamic nation state there is no **civil law**. The law that is enforced on the populace is **religious (Sharia) law**. Sharia law extends to what Western people would consider personal life. Sharia law directs how a person dresses, and how men and women interact with each other.

In classic Islam, the **church is the state**.

The police enforce religious law, and court judgment is made under religious law. There is no difference between **civil (man's) law** and **religious (Allah's) law**. The purpose of the Islamic state is to protect, defend and enforce religious law.

In our American republic, the church and state are separate, but they depend on each other. **The American church depends on the state to protect and defend its right to exist**. The American church has no police department or court system. It doesn't have a military. It depends on our civil government for protection.

On the other hand, the state (the government) depends on the church for the moral training of its citizens. The state and the church have different, but equally necessary, roles to play.

It is the function of the church to give a person a blueprint of how to live a moral life. John Adams signed our Declaration of Independence. He wrote the Massachusetts State Constitution. He was our first Vice President under George Washington, and our second President.

In 1789, about the time our Constitution was ratified, he said: "Our Constitution was designed for a moral and religious people ... it is wholly inadequate to govern any other." Adams was recognizing the essential role faith plays in our Constitutional Republic. Liberty depends on morality. A moral and religious people do not require many civil laws. An immoral people can't pass enough laws to govern themselves.

In Christianity, **the church and state are separate**. But both are a necessary part of self-government.

It is the function of the church to **prevent crime**. It is the function of the state to **punish crime**. *Thou shalt not steal* is a **moral law**. Grand theft auto is a **civil crime**. The only reason the state can give you to **not** steal is: you might be caught and punished.

If this is the reason young people are given for not stealing, they will work harder at not getting caught. If they are God-fearing, they take it on faith that they will get caught every time. Christianity teaches **government of the self**. Conscience is always around, even when the police aren't.

You have probably noticed that the Communists, the Socialists and the Islamic Fascists are getting really chummy. It would seem that an atheistic Communist, a secular Socialist and an Islamic Fascist wouldn't have much in common. There is an old adage that "the enemy of my enemy is my friend." **Their common enemy is individual liberty**.

It is **liberty, not democracy** that will lower the level of friction. When the day comes that the average Muslim wants liberty for himself and he is willing to grant liberty to his neighbor, we will be on the road to peace.

Some Americans believe democracy will magically solve our differences and bring peace to the Middle East. The Palestinians used democracy to elect Hamas, a terrorist organization. On the other hand, Morocco and Jordan are relatively moderate Islamic kingdoms. Better a moderate kingdom than a radical democracy.

There are three major faiths today:

Communism – Where the **state** is the **church**. (Faith in man.)

Islam – Where the **church** is the **state**. (Religious government.)

Christianity – Where the **church and state are separate** but they rely on each other.

Of these three major faiths, only Christianity is compatible with economic, spiritual and personal liberty. Jesus Christ offers salvation. There is no requirement that you accept Him. Our Constitution provides tolerance of people of all faiths....or no faith.

There are no similar guarantees of spiritual or personal liberty in Islamic nations. The communist nation eliminates private property. The socialist/fascist state acquires what property it can, and controls the property it hasn't yet acquired.

There are three major faiths in the world today: Christianity, communism, and Islam. Of these, only Christianity affords economic liberty to the individual person **and** spiritual liberty to his soul.

Sure there are counterfeit Christians. Some are self-righteous, judgmental and "holier than thou." And they commit crimes from time to time. The fact that there are counterfeit Christians just proves the existence of real ones. No one would counterfeit $100 bills if there weren't genuine $100 bills.

If the God of Abraham, Isaac and Jacob is removed from America, **He** will survive. The great "I Am" does not depend on us, it is we who depend on Him. America is a Judeo-Christian nation that tolerates people of other faiths or no faith.

Faith should give one a purpose for living, and a peace about dying ... not an excuse to murder.

"Of these three major faiths, only Christianity is compatible with economic, spiritual **and** personal liberty."

16
Yes, There Really is a Religious Left

Until I served in Congress, I didn't know there was a religious left. I always heard the media talk about the **Christian Right** or "right-wing Christians."

I thought when I began writing this book that I had discovered the **religious left** while I was still a member of Congress. For the heck of it, I googled "**religious left**". Boy was I surprised!

I found a section in Wikipedia called: **Alliance of the Left and Christianity**. It begins: "Starting in the late 19th century (late 1800s) and early 20th century (early 1900s) some began to take on the view that 'genuine' Christianity had much in common with a **leftist** perspective."

This coincides with the establishment of the Fabian Society. The Fabian Society was born in 1893 about the time Karl Marx died. Marx wrote in The Communist Manifesto the following statement: "In this sense, the theory of the **Communists** may be summed up in the single phrase: **Abolition of private property**."

The "basis" for the Fabian Society began: "The Fabian Society consists of **Socialists**. It, therefore, aims at the reorganization of society by **the emancipation of land and industrial capital. From individual and class ownership** ... the society accordingly works for the **extinction of private property in land**."

This is why I said in Chapter 5 that the basic difference between **communism** and **socialism** is the difference between **bullets** and **ballots**. They are going to the same destination. They just ride in different vehicles. The Communist arrives in a tank, the Socialist in a limousine.

The Fabian Society used two methods to further the goals of delivering land and industrial capital (private property) into government hands. One was called **penetration** and its twin was **permeation**. **Penetration** meant getting Socialists into elective and appointed positions of influence. **Permeation** meant convincing someone who was not necessarily a Socialist to do something Socialists wanted done.

In the early 1900s, a Christian book club was started in England by a member of the Fabian Society. Members of this Christian book club were offered most selections of the Left Book Club at discounted prices. The idea was to lead Christians down the path to socialism by appealing to their belief in brotherhood and looking after the less fortunate in society. **The Socialists set out to penetrate and permeate churches as well as educational institutions, media and government**.

What is amazing to me is that practically all of this left-wing philosophy is imported from "the old country." Robert Owen is generally credited with coining the term "Socialist" in the middle of the 19th century in England.

Socialists and Christians are not typically very chummy. In fact, Owen, like most folks on the left, was not a believing Christian. Karl Marx was a committed atheist (denied the existence of God).

Owen brought his ideas of creating a Utopian Socialist Society to America. He bought Harmonie, Indiana, from George Rapp and changed its name to New Harmony. In two years time it failed, and two years later it was dissolved.

Josiah Warren was one of the participants in the New Harmony Society. **He said he believed its failure was caused by the lack of private property and individual liberty**. Duh!

Some sell socialism by claiming that capitalism isn't fair. In a country as wealthy as America, no one should be sleeping on a park bench or in a tent. Young people are particularly idealistic in this regard.

In one of the eighth-grade classes I taught, I began with a question: "Do you believe it is possible for the least intelligent person in this classroom to earn an 'A' in this course?"

No one volunteered an answer. I called on one student.

"Yes, I think it is possible."

"How would he do that?"

"He would have to work harder."

"So, he wouldn't have as much free time for fun?"
"Yes."

"Do you think it is possible for the most intelligent person in this classroom to fail the course?"

"Yes" – everyone agreed.

"How would he do that?"

"That's easy, just don't do anything."

"How would you feel if you were the first person we talked about? You studied hard and long. You missed out on a lot of fun. You earned an 'A'. But, the teacher said it wouldn't be fair for anyone to fail the course. So she said, 'I'm taking a portion of your "A" and giving it to the person that failed the course. You will get a "B" and the person that failed will get a "D" instead of failing.'"

The students thought that was really unfair. The person who wasn't as smart, but worked hard to earn an "A" should receive an "A". I told them, "Welcome to real life, when you complete your education and go to work. If you are blue collar and you work overtime at time and a half or double time; if you are white collar and make smart investments; if you are an inventor who designs a better machine or process – government will take a portion of your economic 'A' and pass it on to those who failed the course. And the more you make, the more they take."

In other words, the harder you work, the more they take from you and pass it on to others. The motto of these Socialists was "from each according to this ability, to each according to his need." Sounds like a really good, moral, almost perfect society.

The problem is that socialism and communism fail any time they are permitted to do so. When was the last time you remember a United States citizen getting picked up at sea, in a makeshift boat, trying to get to Cuba? The Old Berlin Wall was designed to keep people in communist East Germany, not to keep people out.

Stalin had a not-so-flattering term for people who were sympathetic to communism. People who were non-Communists, yet helped the Communist cause, were called "useful idiots." These are people who were manipulated into helping Communists out of idealism.

Do not expect a Socialist to walk around with a sign around their neck saying, "I'm a socialist." In fact, you should expect him or her to deny it. The best you will get is when someone on the left will say they are a **liberal** or a **progressive**.

You must watch what they do. When I visit someone in their home or in their office, the first thing I do is look for a bookcase. You can tell a lot about a person by what they read. You can learn something about them from the company they keep and the causes they embrace.

If you have a priest or a pastor that likes to talk a lot about **social justice** or **economic** issues from the pulpit, you probably have yourself a political lefty. If your minister sticks to **moral** issues, you probably have one from the right.

If you have a priest or a pastor that does not preach on anything controversial, you belong to a Christian country club. The Christian country club set does not want to make anyone uncomfortable; it is bad for business. There are many Jewish country clubs as well.

What the left likes to call **social issues** are really **moral issues**. Traditional marriage and abortion are examples of moral issues. In order to subscribe to the philosophy of the left, a minister would have to become more secular, and less Biblical.

Remember, you either have faith in God or faith in man. Our Founders did not trust people. They knew power had a tendency to corrupt people. They wanted to make sure no one person had too much power.

This is why we have separate legislative, executive and judicial branches within the federal government. Power is further separated between the federal government and individual state governments.

The philosophy of people on the political left is to give government more power and control, and to shrink individual liberty. Jesus Christ offered each of us the gift of salvation. He did not require anyone to take it.

Whether your faith is based on grace or works, it is still about liberty. You are at liberty to accept His grace or not; and you are at liberty to perform good deeds and works, or not.

Yes, there really is a religious left. I am sorry to say I had not discovered them until recently. They have been around a long time. I just didn't notice them before. I included them here because you probably didn't notice them either.

17

The Greatest Hazard to our Separation of Church and State is the Religious Left

Hugo Chavez, the socialist dictator in Venezuela, recently said, "Jesus Christ was a socialist." This is a major shift in attitude for anyone on the far political left. Communism was "invented" by Karl Marx and Frederich Engles in the middle of the 19th century. They were atheists. Since the middle 1800s the classic communist state was the church.

Since communism was itself a faith – faith in man – Communists didn't want any competing faith in God. According to *The Communist Manifesto*, "**Communism abolishes eternal truths, it abolishes all religion and all morality**." The classic Socialist normally subjects faith in God to death by a thousand cuts. For the most part, the Socialist wages a propaganda war and works to undermine the church.

The classic Socialist attempts to undermine the church with legislation, lawsuits and ridicule. They file suit to take God out of the Pledge of Allegiance. They file suit to ban the Ten Commandments from public display. They make public ridicule of faith. They characterize it as something for "weak-minded" people.

The classic Socialist uses legislation and elections, ridicule and public policy to minimize or destroy the church in a "peaceful" fashion. Here we are speaking of the Judeo-Christian tradition, the primary American faith.

Like most Christians, I have what people of faith call a "church home." Most Christians attend the same church every Sunday. In fact, you will normally find them sitting in the same pew. They are creatures of habit. About the only time a typical Christian will visit several churches is when they are searching for a different church home.

Just like your personal residence, you come home to the same house, you tend to sit on the same chair, you are not normally visiting a lot of different houses. When a Christian moves their personal residence, they may begin looking for a new "church home." Or, they may have a growing family. They may look for a church that has better facilities and programs for children.

I have attended "Bible-based" churches for most of my adult life. These are churches where you find what the press calls "the Christian Right." These are people who love God and country. In fact, my home church, Graceland Baptist in New Albany, Indiana, has an annual **"God and Country"** Sunday service to honor U.S. Armed Forces veterans, as do many other churches.

When our local National Guard unit, the 151st (now 152nd) Infantry Battalion, was deployed to Afghanistan, Graceland sent clothing, supplies and money to be distributed to the Afghanis by our soldiers. The 151st was my former unit, and it was my honor to visit them in Afghanistan while they were deployed there. The Christian Right supports the military, their families and the state. **They see no conflict between patriotism and Christianity**.

While I was a member of Congress, I was asked to meet with a ministerial association in a city in my

Mike preparing to board an Army Blackhawk while visiting our soldiers.

district. I incorrectly assumed that all the members of the ministerial association were Christians who held similar beliefs, who were kindred souls. They were quick to inform me that the federal budget was "immoral." We were not building enough public housing for the poor. The Congress was being "immoral" with taxes and appropriations. In effect, they said, **we didn't tax enough, or spend enough to adequately look after the poor**.

I told them I was just a layman, they were the people of the cloth. They certainly knew scripture better than I did. I reminded them of the Bible story about the Good Samaritan; about gleaning (leaving a portion of the harvest in the fields for the poor); about loving thy neighbor as you love yourself; about looking after the widows and children. **Apparently, I missed the part where Christ said you should take from one person at gunpoint and give to another**. I thought charity was voluntary.

A few seconds of silence followed. Then one of them responded, "That is not what we are talking about."

"No," I responded, "that is exactly what we are talking about. If you don't think so, stop paying your taxes. **I assure you that someone will show up with a gun and a badge and take by force whatever the government is owed**."

The religious left seems to believe that government is a non-denominational faith, and taxes are the equivalent of tithing. There was a time in English history when the church was established by the state, and tithing was required by law. This is what the Founders wanted to avoid when they enacted the First Amendment of the United States Constitution.

The religious left believes charity should be enforced, not solicited. They want the state to relieve them of the moral obligation to help the poor. Their consciences are soothed by lobbying the government. You can see it statistically in the recent book Who Really Cares (Arthur C. Brooks). **Being liberal means being liberal with someone else's money, not your own**.

Recently, I was stopped by a guy in a convenience store one night. He was driving a small U-Haul truck. He had his wife and three kids in the cab. He told me he was going to Michigan. He was $5 short of having enough to rent a room for the night. I gave him a $20. He said, "Thanks. That will buy our breakfast in the morning, too." I still feel bad. I should have given him $100.

As a Christian, I feel a moral obligation to help when I can. I do not keep track of all my contributions.

I deduct some from my income; a lot of it goes unnoticed and unreported. These contributions have been made from voluntary action, not a legal requirement. It is written, "God loves a cheerful giver." There is nothing cheerful about paying taxes.

When I read the comments from Hugo Chavez, stating Jesus Christ is a Socialist, then listen to the American religious left and listen to American political candidates on the left, I see an unholy alliance beginning to firm up between the religious left and the political left.

Christ said, "Render unto Caesar what is Caesar's and render unto the Lord what is the Lord's" (Matthew 21:25). The greatest hazard to the separation of church and state lays not with Christian icons or Ten Commandment displays, it's the money.

I disagreed with President Bush on his "Faith-Based Initiative." Government never passes out money without strings. If faith-based organizations become dependent on government funding, they will have to comply with government regulations. In the long run, **government money will corrupt the church**.

Churches are becoming more and more secular today. They do not want to give their congregations any bad news. They want to make people "feel good." Many are becoming religious country clubs. They do not want to make church members squirm in the pews. They want them to work out in the gym.

It is easier for religious and not-for-profit leaders to lobby the government for money than to ask citizens for it. It has two distinct advantages:

1) Government doesn't have to ask for voluntary contributions, they can take it by force of law.

2)   If the voluntary contributor thinks their money is not being spent well, they can stop giving, or go to another church. The taxpayer does not have that option.

My position on separation of church and state earned me the wrath of the religious left. Ministers appeared in campaign commercials, and my opponent sent out flyers basically telling folks I was a bad Christian. These were political pieces disguised as reports on faith. One was headlined, "The Guiding Light" and another as "A Faith and Family Report."

A merger of the political left and the religious left runs the risk of creating the Judeo-Christian equivalent of Islam – or the spiritual equivalent of communism. When the church is the state or the state is the church, individual liberty is lost. I think I understand the proper role of church and state. God will be my judge.

18
Money for Nothing

Money for nothing ...
(Dire Straits)

Government **prints** money just like a casino issues chips. Both of them depend on someone else to create wealth, they just move it around.

The casino depends on **losers** to keep the lights turned on and the doors open. Government depends on **winners** (taxpayers) to meet its payroll.

Geraldo Rivera said **free money** at least three times when talking about the "cash for clunkers" program on television. From time to time I hear an ad offering to help people to get **free government money**.

Here is a news flash: **Government doesn't have any money**. Money can't be **made** by **printing it**. It has to be made the old-fashioned way – someone has to **earn** it.

It is true that government can print more money than is necessary to replace worn out, lost or destroyed money. But if thcy issue new money faster than our economy grows, it causes **inflation**.

Remember Adam Smith's idea about **supply and demand**? It applies to money, too. If the planet is flooded with dollars, they aren't worth as much, which means things will cost you more dollars.

Government gets its money much like you do, with one big exception.

You can get money by **selling something you own**. So can government. California just had a yard sale the other day. They sold surplus stuff, things they weren't using.

Government can **borrow** money. You may have borrowed money to buy a house or a car. In your case, the lender holds the title to the asset (item) you bought until you have paid for it.

In your case, the lender has an appraisal made, or looks at the value of the asset. In the case of a government, they look at the economy of that city, state or country's area.

The other way you have to get money is to **earn** it. This is the big difference between you and your government: You must **earn** the money; **government has the ability to take money from people who earned it**.

There was a guy named Herbert Spencer who bundled up some essays (writings) about government and economics. His 19th-century book The Man vs. The State talked about how people make a living. He said there are only two ways for a person to get his daily bread and keep a roof over his head. One was by the "**fruits of his own labor**." In other words, you earn your own living. The other, he says, was by "**the forced acquisition of the labor of others**." In other words you made a living by taking part of what someone else earned.

He said the former (by one's own labor) should be called the **economic** means of making a living. And the latter (by the forced acquisition of the labor of others) the **political** means of making a living.

I'm from farm country, so we will use that as an example of what Mr. Spencer was talking about. Old McDonald farms the ground and raises farm animals to make his living. He sells his farm products to earn his money.

Local government takes part of Old McDonald's labor (represented by the money he earned) in taxes. So the people in the local government make their living by "**the forced acquisition of the labor of others**." In other words, they make their living by the **political means**. The state and federal governments take from Old McDonald's labor as well.

Remember what Adam Smith said about anyone who, "produces more than they consume" making a nation wealthier? The farmer **produces more than he consumes**. Part of that surplus is taken from him to provide a living for people who **consume more than they produce**.

The bureaucrats today show government job growth as part of our employment statistics. They have economists that will back them up. Some guy said once, "If all the economists in the world were laid end to end, it probably would be a good thing." The London School of Economics, by the way, was started by Fabian Socialists.

Here is the problem, folks. The number of people who make their living by the **economic means** (taxpayers) is shrinking. And the number of people who make their living by **political means** (tax users) is growing.

This is not rocket science. More government employees and people living off of government is not a good thing.

Let's think of this another way. Picture our country as a giant wagon. People who make their living by the **economic means** are pulling the wagon. People who make their living by the **political means** are riding in the wagon.

What happens to our economy, and our country, when everybody decides to sit in the wagon? Why would anybody believe creating more government jobs is a good thing?

We are creating more tax users and eliminating taxpayers. Our President says the people left pulling the wagon are just going to have to pull harder. My granddad said, "You can shear a sheep many times; you can only skin 'em once."

I know some bureaucrat is going to read this and blow a gasket. The first sign that you have become a bureaucrat is when you begin to mistake **activity for production**. I'm not saying that all people who make their living by the **political means** are lazy.

What I am saying is this: The lumberjack that harvested the trees, the employee at the saw mill, the employee at the paper mill, all worked in **producing paper**.

Paper is a product. Shuffling paper is an activity. People who make their living **producing paper** are making their living by the **economic means**. People who **shuffle paper** for the government make their living by the **political means**.

Some non-productive jobs are necessary in a business or a society. In business we call that overhead and we try to keep that at a minimum. Growing government jobs is adding overhead to our nation's economy. It isn't a positive thing. It's something to worry about.

Money for nothing? No, somebody had to earn it, or get it from somebody who did.

"Government doesn't have any money.
Money can't be **made** by **printing it**.
It has to be made the old-fashioned
way – someone has to **earn** it."

19

The United States Constitution Says What It Says – Period

The United States Constitution provides for its own Amendment. An amendment is a legal, proper way to change what the Constitution says. Basically, it is a method to change our country's rulebook.

A federal judge cannot amend (change) our Constitution. All nine judges that sit on the U.S. Supreme Court cannot amend our Constitution, **even with a unanimous decision**. One hundred percent of our United States Representatives, 100 percent of our United States Senators, and the President of the United States **combined** cannot amend our Constitution.

Article V of the United States Constitution provides for two methods of legally amending (changing) our Constitution.

The more common method is: Two-thirds of the United States House of Representatives and two-thirds of the United States Senate propose an amendment; and three-fourths of the state legislatures (38 states) have to ratify (approve of) the proposed amendment for it to become effective.

The other method is: Two-thirds of the state legislatures (34 states) must call for a convention to propose amendments. Any amendments proposed would still have to be ratified by three-fourths of the state legislatures (38 states) before the Constitution is amended.

Many people on the political left do not like our Constitution. Some say our Declaration of Independence and the United States Constitution were written by dead, white male hypocrites. After all, in 1776 we still had slaves, and women did not have the right to vote.

It took about 100 years to build the National Cathedral in Washington, D.C. That does not mean the blueprints were defective. Three generations of the same family of stonemasons worked on the structure – the ones who started it did not live to see it finished.

The biggest problem the left has, with both our U.S. Constitution and the state constitutions, are that they are a big stumbling block for them. The constitutions limit government power. This limits their ability to convert private property into government property.

The Fifth Amendment of the United States Constitution says in part, "... **nor shall private property be taken for public use without just compensation**." So, they cannot just take the farm because they want to. And government must pay for it if they need to build a road on it, or have some other need for it.

There is a story told about how to capture a whole herd of wild hogs. First, you find a good spot to put out some tasty food for them. Once they get comfortable coming to that spot regularly, put up **one side** of a fence big enough to contain the whole herd. Once they are comfortable eating with one side of the fence up, **add a second side**. When they are comfortable with two sides, **add a third**. Finally, **add the last side with a gate installed**. When they are comfortable feeding in the pen, slam the gate shut. They may squeal for awhile, but they have forgotten how to find food on their own anyway.

The Fabian Socialists have a turtle for a logo: MOVE SLOW AND STRIKE HARD. They are patient. They have been building our fence for years, indeed for decades.

We now have a government passenger railroad: AmTrac. Virtually every major city has a local government transit bus and/or light rail line. We now have Government Motors manufacturing cars, and they are running as hard as they can to take over healthcare.

The left always paints a pretty picture of how much better things will be when government takes a more active role. They always make it sound so helpful, so generous, so moral. Don't pay any attention to that fence, they say.

While we were busy making a living by the **economic means**, the left was busy **penetrating** and **permeating** all of our institutions. Most of the left has learned to make their living by the **political means**. They are paid by taking the labor of others by force of law.

In her book *Fabian Freeway* written in 1966, Rose L. Martin notes: "As the British Fabian philosopher, John Atkinson Hobson, had foretold, **the university professor would become the secret weapon of Socialist strategy** on a broader scale than ever before."

The law schools are not exempt. There is no attempt to maintain any diversity of thought in the vast majority of educational institutions. They want diversity of appearance (race, color, sex, etc.), but they are looking for conformity of thought. In other words, they want the same stuff packaged in different-looking containers.

I have carried a pocket copy of the United States Constitution for years. I have given away thousands of them. People have heard about the separation of church and state for so long, they are surprised to learn that the Constitution does not say that.

I was standing in the well of the House Chamber one night between votes. (The "well" is the flat area between the Speaker's rostrum and the first row of seats). There was a lot of discussion going around at the time about the Iraqi Constitution (or lack of one).

One of my former colleagues said: "Well, just **give 'em ours. We aren't using it anymore**." Unfortunately, that has been another strategy of the new left of American politics.

If you cannot get a judge, or panel of judges, to say it says something different than the Founders intended, just ignore it and hope nobody notices. Or, if somebody notices, hope they do not have enough courage or resources to file a Constitutional lawsuit.

Folks, the United States Constitution is the only thing standing between you and the snobs, or the mob. It says what it says – period, until it is legally amended.

As we stated in an earlier chapter, the British "democracy" and the American Republic have entirely different DNA. At Runnymeade, England, in 1215, the English King John **gave limited power to the English**

people. At Philadelphia in 1787, the American people **gave limited power to the American government**.

The left has a theory called **"the inevitability of gradualism."** Over time, the British monarchy ceded more and more of its power to the people. Over time, the American people have ceded more and more of their liberty to their government.

Because the king's power was absolute, the British Parliament's power is absolute. The representatives of the people can do whatever they want. They can (and have) changed the British Constitution.

The American Constitution has proved a major stumbling block to the absolute power of the federal government. About 100 years ago (1913), the American people were convinced to adopt the 17th Amendment to the U.S. Constitution. This started the ball rolling towards a **national** government, rather than a **federal** government.

The U.S. House of Representatives is often called "the people's house." Members are elected to the U.S. House by the people in a Congressional district determined by population.

The U.S. Senate consists of two Senators from each state **regardless of population**. In our Republic, the function of the Senate was to represent the states. Senators were originally elected by state legislatures. The Seventeenth Amendment, ratified in 1913, made them popularly elected.

By making them popularly elected, the check and balance between state power and federal power was virtually eliminated. The Senators no longer represent the states. Most of them move to Washington, D.C., and serve for life. This has permitted more and more federal control of every facet of life.

Many of the changes in our Republic couldn't have taken place without first dumbing down the populace. By virtually taking over the government universities, the left taught the teachers that taught K through 12. The teachers then taught the students, and a completely new reality was created.

In this new reality, our **Constitutional Republic with a federal government is becoming an unlimited democracy with a national government**. Our children are taught in government schools and universities that "the majority rules."

Even in the law schools, Lady Justice (the statue representing our legal system) is encouraged to pull her blindfold up. If, in fact, the U.S. Constitution is "a living, breathing document" that needs to be altered to fit the circumstances, then all of our laws are adjustable to fit the situation.

By doing that, we have exchanged the **rule of law** for **rule by people**. This is what the Founders were trying to avoid. The law should be understandable, reasonable and enforceable. If it needs to be changed, it should be changed. Not by a judge or a group of judges, not on a case-by-case basis; it needs to be changed legally, and applied to all equally.

In order to restore our Constitutional Republic you need to understand it and teach it to your children.

You need to understand it so you can elect people who understand it to represent you.

The United States Constitution says what it says – period. And it should be read in concert with our Declaration of Independence.

"One hundred percent of our U.S. Representatives, and one hundred percent of our U.S. Senators, and the President of the United States **combined** cannot amend our Constitution."

20
The Cowbird Doesn't Make Her Own Nest

The cowbird finds a nest some other bird has built. She removes the other bird's eggs and replaces them with cowbird eggs. More often than not, the unsuspecting "foster parent" will hatch the cowbird eggs. The cowbird avoids parental responsibility by passing it off to another bird.

The American Left is stealing our dreams. Socialists do not **dream**, they **scheme**. Liberals are liberal with someone else's money. As former British Prime Minister Margaret Thatcher pointed out, "The problem with socialism is: Sooner or later you run out of other people's money."

When my son Noah was a young boy he asked me once, "Why do you work so hard? What is it about business that makes you want to work so hard?" I told him, "Business is about dreams. You dream some business up, and then you work hard to make it happen."

What I didn't tell him at that age was, "Failure wasn't an option." When you have pledged your home, your car and virtually everything material that you own as collateral for a business loan, it provides a great incentive to work as hard as necessary.

The American left has taken our dreams out of the nest, and replaced them with nightmares. Our children, their children, and their children's children will struggle financially. They will pay the massive debt being created from bailouts, "cash for clunkers," economic stimulus and pork-barrel projects.

If our kids save money, it will evaporate from inflation caused by printing more money. If they work hard to earn money, more and more of what they earn will go in taxes to pay interest on the debt. If they try to start a business, they will drown in a sea of regulation.

My former opponent was a champion of **PAYGO**. PAYGO says any new spending or tax cuts have to be paid for by **tax increases** or **spending cuts** elsewhere in the budget. What this means is: They want taxpayers to **PAY** more, so they can **GO** on spending your money.

It might be helpful here to talk a little about government debt. Why is government debt a bad thing? Almost all of us have mortgages (or have had one) on our homes. Most of us have had car payments to make. So why is government debt so bad?

When **you** borrow money to buy a home, the lender expects **you** to pay the money back. When **you** borrow money to buy a car, the lender expects **you** to pay it back. When government borrows money, **you** get the benefit and **someone else** has to pay the money back. In effect, you borrowed the money to buy a house and you are forcing someone else to make the payments.

Some of this shifting of responsibility happens in this generation. Like the cowbird, **people who don't pay taxes pass their responsibility off to others who are paying taxes**. But a large part of this is shifting the financial burden from one generation to another.

It would be the equivalent of you borrowing the money to buy a house, and requiring your children and grandchildren to pay for it. How will they afford to buy a home for themselves when they have to make the payments on yours?

Americans used to **sacrifice** for their children, now they are **stealing** from them. This generation enjoys the benefits from all this spending, and future generations will get the bill. The so-called "economic stimulus" and "bailouts" are designed to pass the economic pain on to generations to come.

What amazes me is how people can believe that it is impossible for government to go broke. They understand that individuals can go broke. They understand that companies can go broke. But they somehow have this idea that government can borrow more and spend more, and never go broke.

Folks, a big bulldozer can push more stuff out in front than a smaller one. The individual who has the smallest economic bulldozer can "rob Peter to pay Paul" for a while. A company economic bulldozer can push more than an individual can. But even as large as the government's economic bulldozer is, it can only push so much debt out in front before it grinds to a halt.

The worst part of this is what we are doing to our kids. Americans always believed their children would do better than they did. They worked hard to give their kids the opportunity.

What do we tell our children? Get an education and work hard so you can pay off the national debt? Huh?

Wow! You get a free education so you can get a good job to pay off someone else's credit card, make someone else's house payment, and provide the cash for someone else to trade in his clunker. Are you serious?

Unfortunately, there are people, many people, who gave up their liberty years ago. They really don't care how high the tax burden becomes. They don't pay taxes. They don't care if private property is eliminated. They live in public housing. They are cowbirds, content for someone else to build their nest and feed their young. They still vote.

In addition, we have millions who work for government. An increased tax burden to them means bigger staff, more power, more money to spend, higher salaries, and increased importance. Then we have who knows how many consultants who do studies for government. And agencies like ACORN that perform contract services for government. (These are all designed, of course, to make government larger.) They vote, too.

The majority of these folks are very liberal with other people's money. They are constantly developing programs to spend the surplus created by people who make their living by the economic means. What happens when there isn't any surplus? What happens when everyone decides to sit in the wagon? Who is going to pull it?

Government doesn't have any money. Government depends on private citizens and investors to create the surplus that provides government revenues. What happens when the wheels of industry and agriculture grind to a halt?

What happens when the other birds stop making nests?

The cowbird doesn't make its own nest. The political left has taken the dreams out of our nest. They left us nightmares of debt, taxes and red tape.

"The cowbird finds a nest
some other bird built.
She removes the other bird's eggs and
replaces them with cowbird eggs.
The American left has taken our dreams out of
the nest, and replaced them with nightmares."

21
So, Where Are You
On Our Broken Circle?

Do you want **more** government and **less** liberty? Or do you want **less** government and **more** liberty? Do you want to trade your liberty for more security? Who do you think should control your earnings, your property and your earthly possessions? Are you on the left or the right side?

I was talking with a driver one day in the shop. I practiced a lot of MBWA (Management By Walking Around). I don't remember how the conversation started, but I remember everything after he said: "But you're a Republican." I responded, "And you are a Democrat. What do we disagree on?"

I asked him about abortion. He said he was pro life. I asked him about marriage. He said it should be between one man and one woman. I asked him about the right to keep and bear arms. He said he believed in the Second Amendment. Spending? He thought the budget should be balanced.

After running out of issues, we found that we didn't disagree on anything. At that point, I asked him, "What makes me a Republican and you a Democrat?" After thinking he said: "We need a big government to protect us from big business."

I told him, "**Big business isn't going to kill you deliberately**. They are always looking for more customers so they can sell more stuff. They might kill you by accident or negligence. They could sell you a bad tire that blows out and you run off the road and kill yourself. They might sell you some bad food and you get sick and die.

"On the other hand, Joseph Stalin's communist government **deliberately killed more than 20 million Soviet citizens**. Adolph Hitler's fascist government **killed more than six million** Jews and millions of other European civilians. Mao Zedong's communist government killed **more than 60 million Chinese** ... deliberately."

I told him, **"If I were you, I would be more worried about big government than I would about big business."**

Even General Motors (now Government Motors), as big as they were, **couldn't force me to do business with them**. The government can. Even Microsoft, as big as they are, **can't take my money against my will**. The government can.

So, how much control do you want to give to your government?

"Ozzie" Jones and I were standing in the parking lot one day talking when he came back off a chartered coach trip. "Ozzie" was a former Marine, and drove a motor coach for our company for many years. He took his job seriously ... but not much else. He was always laughing. He is now deceased.

Out of nowhere he asked me: "How does it feel to own all this?"

"All what?"

"All these trucks, tractors and trailers, buses, buildings ... all this stuff."

I chuckled and responded, "Ozzie, I don't really **own** anything. **I just look after this stuff while I'm here**. When I'm gone someone else will have to look after it."

"We both came into this life naked and broke. And we are both going out in a box and a cheap suit. Besides, God doesn't judge you by how much stuff you've got."

The **Communist and the Socialist** are all about **government ownership**. The **Fascist** is about **government control**. We bent the ends of our political graph up until they almost touched. Why? Because **ownership and control are so close to being the same thing**.

In some ways **control is actually better than ownership**. If I offered you a car with a clear title. A car you own outright. But, I can tell you when you can drive it, who can ride in it, and where you can go in it.

Or, if I offered you a leased car you will never own. You can, however, use the leased car anytime you want, go where you want, and take who you want. You would probably choose to **control** the leased car rather than to **own** the other car.

Don't expect any politician to stand up and tell you that they are on the left side of our broken circle. Once in a while one of them will admit to being a progressive or a liberal.

The fact is, the folks on the left side of our broken political circle favor a bigger government. **They want either more government control or more government ownership of our country's assets**.

Figure 4

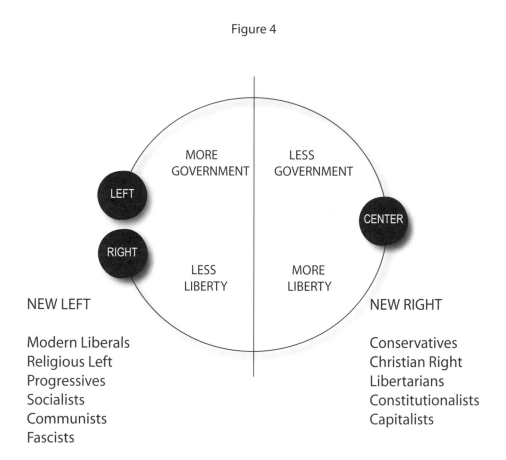

NEW LEFT

Modern Liberals
Religious Left
Progressives
Socialists
Communists
Fascists

NEW RIGHT

Conservatives
Christian Right
Libertarians
Constitutionalists
Capitalists

The purpose of this book isn't to tell you what to think. The purpose is for you to understand your choices. You need to understand the terms and the words used.

Don't misunderstand, I'm no fan of big business. People who work for them tend to develop a mob mentality. They rarely ask:"Is this the right thing to do?" More often they ask:"Is this legal?" Which is like asking:"Can we get away with this?"

Small businesses, and privately held companies, tend to reflect the morals and values of their owners. Publicly traded corporations, both domestic and multinational, are largely amoral and value neutral.

In big business, morality, right and wrong, are replaced by legal, illegal and loopholes, much like big government. But, unlike big government, big business lacks the power to use physical force to impose its' will.

Lord Acton was an English admiral and philosopher. He was the one who said, "Power has a tendency to corrupt; absolute power corrupts absolutely." You need to always keep this in mind.

Our Founders understood this. They took great pains to limit government power, and to check and balance the power given to government. They also understood the Constitution was just words on a piece of paper without Americans who would abide by it, protect it and defend it.

It is up to each generation of Americans to decide how much liberty they want, and what it is worth. So, where are you on our broken circle?

"Even General Motors
(now Government Motors),
as big as they were, **couldn't force me
to do business with them**. The
government can. Even Microsoft, as
big as they are, **can't take my money
against my will**. The government can."

22
For Me It's Still About Liberty

Between a million and a million and a half Americans have **died for liberty**.

They died in our Revolutionary War to **secure liberty** for themselves and the Americans who would come after them.

They died in our Civil War to **extend liberty** to those who did not enjoy its benefits.

They died in WWI and WWII to **restore liberty** to those who had lost it to aggression.

They died in Korea, Vietnam, Iraq, Afghanistan and around the world to **defend liberty**.

What we secured, extended, restored and defended with blood and bullets, we are about to lose with ballots. We are about to lose it from lack of understanding.

We inherited this nation from people who valued liberty above life itself. Listen again to the words of revolutionary patriot Patrick Henry: "I know not what course others may take, but as for me **give me liberty or give me death**."

The New Hampshire State flag still proclaims **"LIVE FREE OR DIE."** The Virginia State flag shows **liberty holding down the tyrant**. It says in Latin, *Sic Semper Tyrannus* – **"Thus always to tyrants."** We used to understand liberty. The American Legion was formed in 1919 at the conclusion of WWI. I am a life member.

If you are a member, get your membership card out. On the back of it you will find the Preamble to the Constitution of the American Legion. For those of you who are not members, I quote in part:

"For **God and Country** we associate ourselves together for the following purposes: **To uphold and defend the Constitution** of the United States of America; to combat the **autocracy of both the classes and the masses**."

The Founders of our country were tired of being governed by kings and queens and royalty (the classes). On the other hand, they did not trust mob rule (the masses). In fact, they did not want to be ruled by people at all.

The definition of the word autocracy: au/toc/ra/cy (ô tä′kra sē) *n.* 1a. Government by a single person having unrestricted power; 1b. A country or a state that has such a government. 2. **Absolute authority; unlimited power or influence in any sphere or group of persons**. 3. Obsolete, independent power.

If you wanted to be a knight in medieval Europe you took an oath to protect and defend your king, with your very life if necessary.

In order to be an American knight (i.e., a soldier, sailor, marine or airman in our United States military), you take an oath to protect and defend **"the Constitution**

of the United States from all enemies foreign and domestic."

In a monarchy (rule by one person), **the king is the highest law of the land**. In an oligarchy (rule by a group), **the majority is the highest law of the land**. In our republic, **the United States Constitution is the highest law of the land**.

Article II, Section 1 of the U.S. Constitution applies to our President. It says, in part, "Before he enter on the execution of his office, he shall take the following oath or affirmation: "I do solemnly swear (or affirm) that I will faithfully execute the Office of President of the United States, and **will to the best of my ability, preserve, protect and defend the Constitution of the United States**."

Article VI of the United States Constitution states: "The Senators and Representatives before mentioned, and the members of the several State Legislatures, and all executive and judicial officers, both of the United States and of the several states **shall be bound by oath or affirmation, to support this Constitution**."

In this book, I have tried to make things as simple to understand as possible. I tried to get an idea down to one or two words. I want adults to be able to share this with their kids. I would like for children to be able to read it.

My one-word definition for the United States Constitution is "**liberty**." Our Constitution restrains our government, and it restrains the majority. In many other governments, **individuals exist to serve the gov-**

ernment. In our system, **government exists to serve the individual**.

I hope this book in some small way will contribute to a new appreciation of our individual liberty and our form of government. Before closing this chapter, I want to share what is arguably the most famous war poem ever written:

In Flanders Fields

In Flanders fields the poppies blow
Between the crosses row on row
That mark our place; and in the sky
The larks still bravely singing, fly
Scarce heard amid the guns below

We are the dead. Short days ago
We lived, felt dawn, saw sunset glow
Loved and were loved, and now we lie
In Flanders fields.

Take up our quarrel with the foe;
To you from failing hands we throw
The torch; be yours to hold it high
If ye break faith with us who die
We shall not sleep, though poppies grow
In Flanders fields.

—Major John McCrae

My maternal grandfather, Dewey Vermillion, was killed in the trenches in France in WWI. He just didn't know it. It took him eight years to die. His lungs never recovered. He was buried the day my mom was born.

Over 400,000 Americans died in WWII alone. There are 9,387 crosses in the American cemetery overlooking the beaches at Normandy, France. This does not count the millions permanently disabled and injured **securing, extending, restoring and defending liberty**.

Will you now break faith with those who died? I will not.

"What we secured, extended, restored and defended with blood and bullets, we are about to lose with ballots. We are about to lose it from lack of understanding."

23

"I Like People Who Can Do Things"

"I like people who can do things."
– Ralph Waldo Emerson

Ralph Waldo Emerson* and his son were trying to get a large calf in their barn. The calf was having none of it. Push and pull as they may, they were not making any headway. A young neighbor girl was watching them. She walked up to the calf and stuck out her finger. When the calf began to suckle her finger she led him into the barn. Emerson walked in the house and wrote seven words in his diary. "I like people who can do things."

Early in my truck driving days I broke down one night just East of St. Louis. St. Louis Mack sent out a mechanic to get the engine running. He arrived at my location in a misting rain. He donned a poncho, picked up four wrenches, a small flashlight, a small cardboard box, stuffed a couple of shop rags in his pocket and walked up to the engine on my unit. While holding the small flashlight in his teeth he located a bad fuel-transfer pump valve and replaced it. I was back on the road 15 minutes after he arrived.

I like people who can do things. This mechanic never made a second trip back to the service truck.

Ralph Waldo Emerson (1803–1882) was an American essayist, philosopher, and poet.

143

From the description of the problem, he determined what was likely to be wrong. He brought everything he needed to fix the problem. There was no lost motion.

We used to be a nation of people who could do things. Indiana's West Baden Springs Hotel was built in 1901. It included the largest free-spanning dome in the world at the time. No one had built a 200-foot free-spanning dome before. **It was built in 200 days**.

New York's Empire State Building was built in 1930 and 1931. It was 1,472 feet tall. No one had built a building that tall before. **It was built in 14 months**. For the next 41 years, it was the tallest building in the world. It held that distinction until the first tower of the World Trade Center was completed in 1972.

We have built transcontinental railroads and highways. Americans invented the light bulb, the telephone, television, the transistor, the airplane and broke the sound barrier. We didn't just do things. We did them bigger, better, faster or more efficiently than ever before.

English is the international language of aviation. Why? Americans such as Wilbur and Orville Wright, Glenn Curtiss, Charles Lindberg and Amelia Earhart pioneered the aviation industry. Americans like Howard Hughes, Chuck Yeager and today's innovators like Burt Rutan have kept America on the leading edge of aviation.

When World War II broke out, the British needed a new fighter plane. North American Aviation said they could deliver a new fighter in four months (120 days).

The result was the P-51 Mustang. Arguably **the most effective fighter of WWII was designed, built and flown within 117 days**.

The United States Army needed a four-wheel-drive vehicle capable of carrying four soldiers or cargo cross-country. The Bantum Car Company **designed and built an operating prototype in 49 days**.

Prior to World War II, Ford Motor Company had never built a long-range bomber. By the war's end, they were producing a four-engine B-24 "Liberator" bomber **every 63 minutes**. More than 8,600 B-24s were produced at Ford's Willow Run plant in Dearborn, Michigan.

The first liberty ship, the S/S Patrick Henry, was built in **244 days**. By the time production ceased, the average time to build one was 42 days. The fastest construction of the 2,751 ships built was the S/S Robert E. Peary. It was launched **four and half days** after the keel was laid.

The Lionel Model Train Company built compasses for the LST (Landing Ship Tanks). The first LST was built in about four months. The last of the 1,051 LSTs produced were completed in two months. The majority were built at "cornfield" shipyards in the Midwest on our inland waterways, many here in Southern Indiana.

Fast forward more than a half-century from World War II. The terrorist attack on the World Trade Center left a hole in the hearts of those who lost loved ones. It also left a physical hole in lower Manhattan. The Empire State Building was built in 14 months. **It has been over**

eight years since 9/11 and the hole at ground zero is still a hole.

President Dwight D. Eisenhower signed the act creating the Interstate Highway System on June 29, 1956. It authorized 41,000 miles of interstate to be built. According to a report prepared for the American Highway Users Alliance, by 1980, 40,000 miles were complete.

I live in New Albany, Indiana, across the Ohio River from Louisville, Kentucky. In the middle 1980s we began the process of trying to get another bridge built across the Ohio River. It was to connect I-265 in Kentucky with I-265 in Indiana. The first study was **completed** in 1987.

Let's put this in perspective. **We built 40,000 miles of Interstate Highway in 24 years**. We built it over mountains and tunneled through mountains. We built overpasses and underpasses, exit ramps and entrance ramps. God only knows how many bridges, over how many rivers, were built in that 24-year period.

Now we can't build **one bridge** over **one river** in 24 years. I assure you the Interstate Highway System could never be built today. Endless red tape, studies and hearings would drain the resources required to build it.

It has been said that the first sign you have become a bureaucrat is when you begin to mistake **activity** for **production**. Today we have thousands of bureaucrats that have no sense of urgency. They are inclined to just say no. We have thousands of consultants that make their living holding hearings, doing studies and recommending more studies.

Our tax system and regulatory system is strangling the life out of our economy. The political left is slowly suffocating the most creative, innovative and successful economy Planet Earth has ever seen.

I like people who are considerate of our environment. I like people who make the best use of our resources. And I like people who produce something and create productive jobs.

Nations become wealthier from citizens who produce more than they consume. America is the most generous nation on earth. It is in the world's best interest for America to be productive and successful.

I like people who can do things. We need more of them. We need more people pulling the wagon, and fewer people riding in it.

"We built 40,000 miles of Interstate Highway in 24 years. Now we can't build **one bridge** over **one river** in 24 years. I assure you the Interstate Highway System could never be built today. Endless red tape, studies and hearings would drain the resourses required to build it."

24
So What Will You Do Now?

They say that knowledge is power. By now you know a **Communist** will take your property with **bullets**. A **Socialist** will take your property with **ballots** and call it social justice. A **Fascist** may let you keep your property, **if you do what you are told to do with it**.

You understand that a **progressive**, a **liberal** and/or the **religious left** all want **more government**, which means **less individual liberty**. You have noticed that our broken circle shown in Chapter 4 does not have Democrats or Republicans on it.

I don't care about the Democrat donkeys or the Republican elephants. I care about my kids, your kids and their kids. I love God and country. I want a smaller government, serious tax reform, a strong defense and fiscal responsibility (balancing the budget).

The tea party demonstrations are a great thing. But do not kid yourself. The "rent-a-mob" crowd will try to eventually wear you out. The majority of the tea party folks have real jobs. They make their living by diligent hard work.

The political left, for the most part, makes their living by political means. They have more time to spend protesting, demonstrating, lobbying, making noise and effecting policy. Moving the country to the left is what they do. And they have been good at **penetration** and **permeation**.

You must set some achievable goals and "git r done," to quote Larry the Cable Guy. It isn't enough to be against something. When the adrenaline of the moment is gone, you will lose the momentum. The left believes in "the inevitability of gradualism." They will take what ground they can and hold it until you are tired. Then they will move again.

I know many of you are not "joiners." You are independent thinkers, and not taken to group action. Like Will Rogers once said, "He wouldn't join any club that would have him for a member." You have to understand that to succeed you must out-organize the community organizers.

You don't have to practice group think, or march in lock step as the left does, but you must coordinate enough to make sure you have covered all your bases. You have to fight the fight on every front, just as they have.

Keep in mind the words of General George C. Patton. He was asked once why he pressed the attack when he was outgunned, outmanned and short on supplies. His response was, "Because I was too weak to defend."

In order to save this nation and individual liberty for you and your posterity, you must shift from defense to offense. We must attack the left everywhere.

As Winston Churchill said in World War II, "We shall fight on the beaches, we shall fight on the landing grounds, we shall fight in the fields and in the streets, we shall fight in the hills; we shall never surrender."

We must take on the political left everywhere we find them: in the halls of government, on the pages of textbooks, on university campuses and by seizing any and all media opportunities. And don't forget the seminaries and lukewarm churches.

We cannot just try to hold a defensive position. We have to go on the offense.

Here are several items worthy of your time, effort and commitment to Churchill's conviction that "We shall never surrender."

1)   *Term limits for the U.S. House and Senate.* We have term limits for the President. We need them for Congress. Maximum five terms in the U.S. House; maximum two terms in the U.S. Senate. We will probably have to make it effective for members elected **after** a certain date. It takes a Constitutional amendment to accomplish this.

2)   *Pass a law that prohibits an increase in the salary or fringe benefits of any member of Congress (U.S. House or Senate) unless the federal budget is balanced.* Follow up with a Constitutional amendment in order to "carve it in stone." May want to include the President, Cabinet secretaries and department heads. Basically everyone in a position to effect spending.

3)   *Enact the FairTax, HR25, and repeal the Sixteenth Amendment of the U.S. Constitution.* The FairTax does not have to wait for repeal of the Sixteenth Amendment (Federal Income Tax). It can be passed with a reversion clause. If any tax is levied under the Sixteenth, or the Sixteenth Amendment is not repealed within 10 years of the passage of HR25, the tax system

151

reverts to that which was in effect on enactment of the FairTax.

4) *Elect "low maintenance" members of the federal, state and local government to represent you.* In business we have low maintenance machines and high-maintenance ones. Either one will do the job, but one requires a lot of attention. If you have an elected representative that must be pressured to do the right thing, replace them. And enact term limits on the state and local government as well.

5) *Lobby for repeal of "enabling legislation."* This is legislation that permits the referees to make the rules. Congress should have to pass the laws and amend the laws. This should not be done through an administrative process that has the force of law. Congress has delegated too much of its authority, and I am not convinced that this regulatory process is Constitutional either.

6) *Divide up the work. Establish tasks.* For example: Letters to the editors (LTEs). You need a group that will keep a steady flow of LTEs on the subject of individual liberty, and legislation/regulation that restricts it. You need good school board members and people to review textbooks for revisionist history. Use people where they are best suited. Use their God-given gifts where they can be most effective.

7) *E Pluribus Unum.* From many, one. You need volunteers to work toward maintaining a common American language and a common American culture. People who **immigrate** to America must be committed to **being** an American. We speak English in America. It is okay if you do not eat pork or drink alcohol. But you must

tolerate people who do. Real **tolerance means** you don't have to like it – you just have to put up with it.

The author of our Declaration of Independence and our third President Thomas Jefferson said: "The price of liberty is eternal vigilance." The people have not been vigilant.

They have given over their children to government schools to be taught whatever is in government's best interest. They have not been vigilant in the education of their children.

They have given their government over to career politicians and bureaucrats. They have not attended city and county council meetings. They have not observed Ronald Reagan's policy of "trust, but verify."

They didn't want to be bothered by politics. It was too ugly for them. They forgot what John Adams, our second President, said: "All of these offices will be filled." If good folks won't, others will.

You must organize yourselves. Everybody doesn't have to do everything, but everybody must do something. Use your God-given talents in the area best suited for you.

Let no school textbook go unread and no facts go unverified.

Let no letter to the editor encouraging bigger government and less liberty go unanswered.

Let no election cycle come and go without having a conservative on the ballot.

Let no errant sermon be preached. Do your own study of scripture. "Where the spirit of the Lord is, there is liberty" (II Corinthians 3:17).

EPILOGUE

We used to sacrifice for our children. Each generation gave up something, so the next generation would have better opportunities. Each generation stood on the shoulders of the generation that went before them.

We used to sacrifice for the next generation. **Now we are stealing from them**. In order to avoid economic pain today, we pushed it off on the next generation and their children.

We have saddled future generations of Americans with crushing public debt. The option is job-killing, economy-crashing taxes, or more likely both crushing debt and taxes.

It is virtually impossible for the counter-revolutionaries in the Executive Branch of the government to make a mistake on such a grand scale. They can not believe they can defy the laws of supply and effective demand.

These people have different motives than restoring the health of a market-driven economy. They have little interest in protecting and defending our liberty, economic or otherwise.

These people believe in government control or ownership of every aspect of life. This makes them part Socialist and part Fascist. I can use those words now that you know what they mean.

You will find two items in the back of this book for those of you that are interested. One is my 2009 Christmas poem. The other is from Cicero written in

Rome in the 1st century B.C. He saw what was coming for Rome.

I know that what I have written on these pages will not set well with many folks in the power structure. The most difficult thing to find in Washington, D.C., is the truth. And it is not well received.

Many people today have been taught that there is no absolute truth; only your truth and my truth. I actually asked a bureaucrat one day in negotiations: "Can we agree that 60 divided by 6 equals 10?"

My question was met with silence. He knew the answer would not support his theory, so he refused to answer.

In contemporary America, science is political and math is political. The '60s mantra "The personal is political and the political is personal" has become common.

Our government schools have dumbed down the populace. The high school drop-out rate is as unbelievable as the public debt. The solution to every problem is to spend more money. The reason for every failure is we didn't spend enough money.

People drinking from the public trough have given up virtually all of their liberty to avoid the stress of fending for themselves. Now they want to take our liberty by force of law to support their programs.

The current administration is making their "enemies" list. They work to silence the few Paul Reveres that ride through our streets and shout over the airwaves that "The Socialists are coming, the Socialists are coming."

The Socialists are here. They sit next to you in the pews on Sunday. They sit around your dining room table with you at Sunday dinner. You work with them every day.

Most of them will not admit to being Socialists. They may call themselves progressives, or liberals, or independents. The real Socialists make sure it is "never called by its right name."

We inherited this country from people who valued liberty above life itself. From Patrick Henry's "Give me liberty or give me death" to the New Hampshire flag's "Live Free or Die."

Thomas Jefferson said, "The price of liberty is eternal vigilance." To be vigilant is to be watchful, be on the lookout. In order to be on the lookout, you must know what to look for.

In nature, animals often camouflage themselves to be difficult to spot in their natural environment. You must know what you are looking for to find the new left. The American left does not wear a sign around their necks, or a name badge.

The American left uses verbal camouflage. They will deny they are what they are. They will change the subject. They will deny they are doing what they are doing. You must know what to watch for in order to be vigilant.

In fact, the Fabian Socialist writer George Bernard Shaw said the Socialists' goal was to be achieved by "stealth, intrigue, subversion, and the deception of never calling Socialism by its right name."

I hope and pray this book has given you the knowledge to know what you are looking for, and the confidence and determination to stand against it. For those of you who are Christians, Galatians 5:1 – "Stand fast therefore in liberty by which Christ has made us free, and do not be entangled again with the yoke of bondage."

For those of you who aren't Christians, I recommend author Ayn Rand. *Anthem* is a short read, *Atlas Shrugged* is her longest, and *We The Living* a window to a communist society. This I will assure you: If you do not read, you will not know. I read both scripture and secular writings.

Sun Tzu wrote in *The Art of War* "know your enemy and you will not lose in a hundred battles." General George Patton read Rommels book. I had to read the Communist Manifesto to understand Communism/Marxism.

I don't know what God has in store for America. None of us had any control over the circumstances of our birth. A few of us are given a choice of our time and place of death. If the day comes that I can no longer live like a free man. I pray God will give me the opportunity, and the courage to die like one.

How the Republic Was Destroyed

A nation can survive its fools and even the
ambitious. But it cannot survive treason from
within. An enemy at the gates is less formidable for
he is known and he carries his banners openly.
But the traitor moves among those
within the gate freely, his sly whispers rustling
through all the alleys, heard in the very halls
of government itself.
For the traitor appears no traitor; he speaks
in the accents familiar to his victims, and he wears
their face and their garments, and he appeals to
the baseness that lies deep in the hearts of all men.
He rots the soul of a nation;
he works secretly and unknown in the night to
undermine the pillars of a city;
he infects the body politic so that
it can no longer resist.
A murderer is less to be feared.

— Cicero

Christmas

On Christmas Day we celebrate
God's Son arrived to change our fate.
God gave us much, all of
Creation,
And He gave us this great
nation.

The price was dear, it wasn't free.
Some gave their life for liberty.
To save your soul, Christ Jesus
died.
So you live free; some mothers
cried.

Compared to pen, the sword
it pales
Unless the thought behind
it fails
To wake our patriots from sleep,
Determined liberty to keep.

When I put my pen to paper,
I always ask and seek God's favor,
But I don't think my fervent prayer
Will cause my pen to float on air.

Some Christians say if we all pray,
That prayer alone will save the day.
Then why would David face Goliath?
His sling and stone he need not tryeth.

Second Corinthians, Three:
One Seven
Says liberty comes down from
Heaven.
Our Founders, they believed that too,
Straight from God to me and you.

This Government has failed to note
What our Founders said and wrote
About the Rights to us God granted,
They think from Government it's
rented.

And this new Landlord has no rules,
He's confident He governs fools.
And like a King from days gone by
Their King's the Law, if you ask
why!

And Five of Nine black robes can't
change
Or alter, twist or rearrange
Words written in our Constitution,
For which we fought a Revolution.

The House and Senate altogether
Can't change a phrase, or just one
letter
In the U.S. Constitution
For which we fought a Revolution.

Poem 2009 ⟨∞∞∞∞∞∞∞∞∞∞∞∞∞∞∞∞∞∞∞∞∞∞∞∞∞∞⟩

Since nine black robes, plus House
and Senate
Can't change a thing that's written
in it,
They ignore our Constitution,
For which we fought a Revolution.

They pretend it doesn't matter,
The rule of Law, just idle chatter.
They herd the sheep and shear 'em,
too.
They'll do it till the sheep are
through.

And when the Spirit leaves the
sheep,
They want his hide, they want the
meat
Of mortal life, a skeleton
Left for the daughter or the son.

Government Motors was the start;
They will control each single part
Of life and every institution.
They will undo our Revolution.

Americans died to make us free.
You understand? Why don't you
see?
It's not our Health Care Institution;
They will undo our Revolution.

What was bought by life and limb
We are placing at the whim
Of Bureaucrats, our
Liberty
We will have none, but Health
Care's free.

To go and hide, there's much temp-
tation;
A daunting task to save
a Nation.
To start one took a heavy price,
Our Founders paid and some paid
twice.

I was tempted, I must admit;
Maybe we will prove unfit
To wear the mantle passed down
to us.
We want things fast, no mess or
fuss.

In '44 on Christmas Day,
Our soldiers they were in the fray,
In the snow and in the fight,
For Liberty to make things right.

So will you fight, or will you hide?
You have to think, you must decide.
Your answer holds a Nation's fate,
If you don't act, until too late.

*"I am the good shepherd.
The good shepherd gives His life for the sheep. But
a hireling, he who is not the shepherd,
one who does not own the sheep, sees the wolf
coming and leaves the sheep and flees; and the wolf
catches the sheep and scatters them.
The hireling flees because he is a hireling and does
not care about the sheep. I am the good shepherd;
and I know My sheep, and am known by My own. As
the Father knows Me, even so I know the Father; and
I lay down My life for the sheep. And other sheep
I have which are not of this fold; them also I must
bring, and they will hear My voice; and there will be
one flock and one shepherd."*

John 10:11-16 NKJV